THE "I LOVE MY AIR FRYER"

Three-Step

RECIPE BOOK

From *Cinnamon Cereal French Toast Sticks* to
Southern Fried Chicken Legs, 175 Easy Recipes
Made in Three Quick Steps

Michelle Fagone
of CavegirlCuisine.com

Adams Media

New York London Toronto Sydney New Delhi

To Sam
We're empty nesters now—can't wait for our next chapter!
Love you, Michelle

Adams Media
An Imprint of Simon & Schuster, Inc.
100 Technology Center Drive
Stoughton, Massachusetts 02072

First Adams Media trade paperback edition June 2022

ADAMS MEDIA and colophon are trademarks of Simon & Schuster.

For information about special discounts for bulk purchases, please contact Simon & Schuster Special Sales at 1-866-506-1949 or business@simonandschuster.com.

The Simon & Schuster Speakers Bureau can bring authors to your live event. For more information or to book an event contact the Simon & Schuster Speakers Bureau at 1-866-248-3049 or visit our website at www.simonspeakers.com.

Photographs by James Stefiuk

Manufactured in the United States of America

1 2022

Library of Congress Cataloging-in-Publication Data has been applied for.

ISBN 978-1-5072-1915-7
ISBN 978-1-5072-1916-4 (ebook)

Always follow safety and commonsense cooking protocols while using kitchen utensils, operating ovens and stoves, and handling uncooked food. If children are assisting in the preparation of any recipe, they should always be supervised by an adult.

Contains material adapted from the following titles published by Adams Media, an Imprint of Simon & Schuster, Inc.: *The "I Love My Air Fryer" Low-Carb Recipe Book* by Michelle Fagone, copyright © 2020, ISBN 978-1-5072-1226-4; *The "I Love My Air Fryer" Gluten-Free Recipe Book* by Michelle Fagone, copyright © 2019, ISBN 978-1-5072-1041-3; and *The Everything® Air Fryer Cookbook* by Michelle Fagone, copyright © 2018, ISBN 978-1-5072-0912-7.

Contents

Introduction

The air fryer is a revolutionary appliance that can save you time, calories, and counter space! It can replace your oven, microwave, deep fryer, and dehydrator *and* cook delicious meals in a fraction of the time you're used to. If you don't have a lot of time to spare, the air fryer is a game changer!

And with *The "I Love My Air Fryer" Three-Step Recipe Book*, breakfast, lunch, dinner, and dessert will be on the table in record time, without lots of ingredients, complicated instructions, and hands-on cooking time.

Featuring 175 quick, easy, and delicious recipes, this book will help make sure you're not spending all of your free time in the kitchen. Soon you'll see there's no need to follow long, detailed, multipage recipes to make great-tasting dishes. You can do it all in just three steps.

You'll also find a chapter that tells you everything you need to know about using an air fryer as well as some basics that will help you find success while trying to cook a meal in record time. You'll learn what kind of air fryer to buy, the best and most efficient ways to use it, and how to clean it quickly and thoroughly.

In just three quick and easy steps, anyone—from true beginners to experienced cooks—can have a satisfying meal on the table. So let's get air frying!

Air Fryer Essentials

The air fryer has become a favorite kitchen appliance for good reason: It cooks foods quicker than the conventional oven, doesn't heat up your living space (which you'll be thankful for on those warm weather days), and is easy to clean. In addition, the air fryer makes fried foods guilt-free! In this chapter, you will learn more about the functions of the air fryer, its helpful accessories, and the benefits of air frying.

Keep in mind that while this chapter covers the basics of using your air fryer, the first step is to read the manual that came with your air fryer. All air fryers are different, and with the recent rise in popularity of the appliance there are a lot of different models on the market. Learning how to use your specific air fryer thoroughly is the key to success and will familiarize you with troubleshooting issues as well as safety functions. Read through the manual and wash all parts of the appliance with warm, soapy water before first use to get ready to unleash your culinary finesse!

Why Air Frying?

Who benefits from owning an air fryer? The answer is everyone! The air fryer works by circulating a constant stream of hot air that cooks food evenly and quickly, crisping up edges as it does its job. This is why the air fryer cooks food quicker than a conventional oven—but the benefits of this appliance don't stop there. Here are a few more reasons to switch to air frying:

It replaces other cooking appliances. The air fryer is the perfect alternative to your oven, but it can also replace your deep fryer, dehydrator, and microwave! In one device, you'll be able to whip up perfect meals, snacks, sides, and more without sacrificing any of the flavor.

It produces better results than a conventional oven when cooking frozen food. You'll find many quick food options in the frozen food aisle, but while the microwave cooks them fast, frozen foods never quite come out as crisp as you would like. The air fryer creates a perfect crunchy exterior.

It uses little to no cooking oil. Traditionally cooked fried foods are prepared by submerging foods in heated oil, which makes them high in fat and calories. Also, when oil is heated beyond its smoking point, as it is with deep frying, it can produce toxic fumes and free radicals. The air fryer drastically cuts down on fatty oils, creating more nutritious meals. This in turn contributes to weight loss and better overall health. If you want to cut back on oil even more when using your air fryer, instead of giving your basket a light spray or brush of oil, simply cut a piece of parchment paper to the size of the bottom of your fryer basket. It will help keep the batter on your items without adding additional calories.

It makes vegetables appeal to the pickiest eaters. Picky vegetable eaters (or parents of picky vegetable eaters) can benefit from the transformative ways of the air fryer. Breading and a fresh dipping sauce will turn that zucchini into tasty fries! And a little potato chip breading on a piece of fish can be your gateway recipe from fish sticks to a salmon fillet.

Purchasing an Air Fryer

Several brands, sizes, and temperature ranges of air fryers can be found on the market. This book is based on a family-sized, 1,700-watt air fryer with a 5.8-quart capacity. If you're looking to cook meals to feed just one or two people, you may be interested in a 5.3-quart fryer that can be used to roast an entire chicken. If you want a small machine because of limited kitchen space and you're cooking smaller batches, you still can crisp up savory Breaded Parmesan Zucchini Fries (see Chapter 4) with a smaller model. Some air fryers allow you to dehydrate foods by cooking them at a very low temperature for a long period of time. Depending on the functions you need, you'll want to make sure your air fryer has the appropriate cooking capacity and temperature range.

Air Fryer Functions

Settings vary among different air fryer models on the market. Some of the newer types offer digital settings to control the temperature and time, while others have analog dials as well as preset temperatures for certain fresh and frozen foods. All recipes in this book were created using manual times and temperatures. Every air fryer allows you to set these yourself. Still, it is important to know how the cooking programs work on your air fryer and when to use them. And although some brands will claim you don't need to preheat the air fryer, skipping this step can alter cooking times. The recipes in this book include preheating instructions.

In addition, because the fryer basket is going to be used when making most of your air-fried foods, finding a model with a quick-release button will make your life easier. This button releases the fryer basket containing food from the bottom basket so you can shake or flip the food with ease.

Air Fryer Accessories

The air fryer comes with a fryer basket, but you'll expand the variety of recipes you can make with the purchase of a few additional accessories. Before you buy any of these, check that they work with your size and brand of air fryer. Here are some of the common air fryer accessories:

- **Metal holder.** This round rack allows for a second layer of food in the air fryer so you can maximize space and cook multiple foods at once.
- **Skewer rack.** Similar to a metal holder, this rack also contains four metal skewers for roasting meat and vegetable kebabs.

- **Ramekins.** Small ramekins are great for making mini cakes and quiches. If they're oven-safe, they're safe to use in your air fryer.
- **Reusable silicone liners.** To avoid using endless squares of parchment paper or aluminum foil, these silicone liners are perfect. Think of them as mini Silpats—instead of protecting your cookie sheet, they act as a barrier in your fryer basket!
- **Cake barrel.** Both round and square versions are available. As a bonus, they have a handle that makes retrieving the barrel from the air fryer a cinch.
- **Cupcake pan.** This pan usually comes with seven silicone cupcake liners (also called muffin cups) that are oven-safe and great for mini meatloaves, cupcakes, on-the-go frittatas, quick breads, and muffins. They are reusable and dishwasher safe, making cleanup a snap!
- **Parchment.** Specially precut parchment paper makes cleanup even easier when baking with your air fryer. You can also find parchment paper with precut holes for steaming.
- **Pizza pan.** This shallow nonstick pan allows you to make mini pizzas and also provides a flat surface for a variety of other recipes such as biscuits and cheesecakes.
- **Grill pan.** This replaces the fryer basket and is used for grilling fish, meat, and vegetables, and baking certain desserts, such as pavlova.

Accessory Removal

When using an accessory in your air fryer, you'll want to be careful to avoid burning yourself when it's time to remove the inserted pan. Here are a few useful tools for safely removing items from your air fryer:

- **Tongs.** Wooden or silicone-tipped tongs will allow you to safely remove pans that don't have handles. They will also help you to flip foods like meat.
- **Oven mitts.** Because of the tight space, it is almost impossible to use thick oven mitts to grip accessories in the air fryer. Heat-resistant mini mitts or pinch mitts are small food-grade silicone oven mitts that will allow you to lift pots out of the fryer safely after the cooking process.

Accessory Removal Hack

You can also create an aluminum foil sling to lift a heated dish out of the air fryer. Simply fold a 10" × 10" square of aluminum foil in half, then fold again lengthwise. Place the sling underneath the bowl or pan before cooking, and lift by the sides of the foil when it's time to remove.

Quick and Easy Cooking Tips

The fact that you have chosen an air fryer means that you are already on board with quick and easy. Whether you are cooking from scratch (and this cookbook has you covered here) or reheating frozen meals, the air fryer will be your go-to appliance. The following are some tips to cut down your time when cooking:

- Purchase prechopped onions or peppers for recipes. You won't need to defrost them. Just add and go!
- Although your fryer basket is most likely dishwasher-safe, cut down some of the mess by lining the basket with

parchment paper, aluminum foil, or silicone mats made specially for air fryers.

- Once a week, prep fresh items such as meatballs or chicken patties and freeze. During the week, these items can be air fried in minutes straight from the freezer for a quick snack or meal.

Cleaning and Seasoning

After using your air fryer, it is important to unplug the appliance and allow it to completely cool before cleaning. Adding cool water to a hot fryer basket can cause warping. Although the removable parts are dishwasher safe, washing them by hand can lengthen the life of the coated nonstick parts. To clean the air fryer pan you'll need to:

1. Remove the air fryer pan from the base. Fill the pan with hot water and dish soap. Let the pan soak with the frying basket inside for 10 minutes.
2. Clean the basket thoroughly with a sponge or brush.
3. Remove the fryer basket and scrub the underside and outside walls.
4. Clean the air fryer pan with a sponge or brush.
5. Let everything air dry and return it to the air fryer base.
6. Wipe the outside of the air fryer base with a damp cloth.

Once dry, the fryer basket will benefit if seasoned. You may have heard this term before in reference to cast iron pans. Preheat the air fryer with the basket for 5 minutes at 400°F. Remove the basket and, when it's cool enough to touch, use a paper towel to spread a thin layer of coconut oil on the inside. Then simply heat the basket for an additional 2 minutes. This will help extend the life of the nonstick coating in the basket.

Now that you know the basics of air frying, the only thing left to do is get started.

2

Breakfast

Everyone has heard it before—breakfast is the most important meal of the day. But somehow it's also the one that gets skimped on when people are short on time. Getting ready for the day, getting the kids on the bus, and getting to work on time can be hectic, to say the least. Breakfast often suffers as a result. Sometimes this means grabbing something from the drive-through or skipping the meal altogether. These aren't the healthiest options. Not to mention that eating at home is easier on the wallet. The good news is that this chapter has plenty of quick breakfast ideas to help add some ease to your mornings and set a positive tone for the rest of the day. Some are even portable so you can grab and go. Start your morning right with choices like Strawberry Muffins, Homemade Granola, or delicious Brekkie Flatbreads!

Breakfast Tortilla Wraps

As you may have seen, the TikTok tortilla wrap craze has the social media world, well, obsessed! If you can think it, you can wrap it, as evidenced by the thousands of influencers showing their version. The great thing is that the air fryer takes this craze to the next level—and you can have a crispy wrap in your hands within minutes.

Hands-On Time: 15 minutes
Cook Time: 4 minutes
Preheat Temperature: 350°F
Preheat Time: 3 minutes
Accessories/Prep: Fryer basket lined with aluminum foil

Serves 4

- 4 (8") flour tortillas
- 4 large eggs, scrambled
- ½ cup shredded Cheddar cheese
- 4 slices cooked bacon, halved

TIKTOK TORTILLA WRAP HACK
If you are a visual person and the steps sound confusing, search online for "TikTok Tortilla Wrap Hack." There are hundreds of visuals available as step-by-step pictures or in video format. Once you get it, it is so easy, and it makes the perfect vessel for a wrap!

1   Place one tortilla on a cutting surface. Using a sharp knife, make a cut from the center of the tortilla to the edge. Imagine dividing the tortilla into four sections with the cut facing toward you. To the bottom left quadrant, add ¼ scrambled eggs. To the top left quadrant, add 1 tablespoon Cheddar. To the top right quadrant, add two bacon halves. To the bottom right quadrant, add an additional 1 tablespoon Cheddar.

2   Fold tortilla as follows to form a triangle: Begin by folding the bottom left quadrant over the top left quadrant; then, proceeding clockwise, fold this triangle over the top right quadrant and finally down over the bottom right quadrant. Repeat with remaining tortillas.

3   Place wraps in prepared fryer basket and cook 2 minutes. Flip wraps. Cook an additional 2 minutes. Transfer to a plate and serve warm.

PER SERVING

CALORIES: 326 | **FAT:** 15g | **PROTEIN:** 17g | **SODIUM:** 702mg | **FIBER:** 1g | **CARBOHYDRATES:** 26g | **SUGAR:** 2g

Smoked Salmon Everything Eggrolls

Channel the flavors of lox and bagels into a perfectly packaged, crispy eggroll. Because these are portable, they're perfect for on-the-go breakfasts. But that doesn't mean you can't enjoy them sitting down. They're a unique addition to Sunday brunch, will be sure to impress your friends, and pair perfectly with a mimosa.

Hands-On Time: 15 minutes
Cook Time: 8 minutes
Preheat Temperature: 325°F
Preheat Time: 3 minutes
Accessories/Prep: Fryer basket sprayed with olive oil cooking spray

Serves 2

- 4 ounces cream cheese, softened
- 1 teaspoon chopped fresh dill
- 1 teaspoon everything bagel seasoning
- ¼ cup finely diced red onion
- 4 eggroll wrappers
- 2 tablespoons drained capers
- 1 medium Roma tomato, seeded and diced
- 4 ounces smoked salmon
- Cooking spray

1 In a medium bowl, combine cream cheese, dill, everything bagel seasoning, and onion.

2 Place an eggroll wrapper on a work surface. Down the middle of each wrapper, evenly layer the cream cheese mixture, capers, tomato, and salmon. Fold ½" of both ends of wrapper over mixture. Roll lengthwise to form an eggrolls and transfer seam side down to a plate. Repeat with remaining wrappers and filling.

3 Place eggrolls seam side down in prepared fryer basket. Spray tops of eggrolls with cooking spray. Cook 4 minutes. Flip eggrolls and spray again. Cook an additional 4 minutes. Transfer to a plate and serve warm.

PER SERVING

CALORIES: 470 | FAT: 20g | PROTEIN: 21g | SODIUM: 2,069mg | FIBER: 2g | CARBOHYDRATES: 43g | SUGAR: 4g

Strawberry Muffins

After picking some strawberries at the patch, these muffins are a tasty way to use your haul (though store-bought berries are perfectly fine too). Fresh and quick, this meal-on-the-go will yield some happy family members! Though they're homemade and sure to impress, they're simple and easy.

Hands-On Time: 10 minutes
Cook Time: 12 minutes
Preheat Temperature: 350°F
Preheat Time: 3 minutes
Accessories/Prep: Fryer basket and 4 lightly sprayed silicone muffin cups

Serves 4

1 cup all-purpose flour
1/3 cup granulated sugar
1 teaspoon baking powder
1/8 teaspoon salt
1 teaspoon vanilla extract
3 tablespoons unsalted butter, melted
2 large eggs
2/3 cup whole milk
1/4 cup finely diced strawberries

DO SILICONE CUPS NEED TO BE GREASED?
As most packaging will claim, the answer is "Not necessarily." However, you can give them a light mist of cooking spray or even line them with festive paper cups, depending on the holiday!

1 In a large bowl, combine all ingredients, but do not overmix.

2 Divide batter evenly among prepared silicone muffin cups.

3 Place muffin cups in fryer basket and bake 12 minutes. Remove from basket to a cooling rack and let cool to room temperature. Serve.

PER MUFFIN

CALORIES: 321 | FAT: 12g | PROTEIN: 8g | SODIUM: 248mg | FIBER: 1g | CARBOHYDRATES: 44g | SUGAR: 20g

Espresso Chip Muffins

Need a little pick-me-up? Look no further than one of these espresso muffins. You can find espresso baking chips in the baking aisle or online. If you'd like to switch it up, don't be afraid to try one of the many varieties of chips and morsels available. They will all work in this simple breakfast muffin recipe.

Hands-On Time: 10 minutes
Cook Time: 7 minutes
Preheat Temperature: 375°F
Preheat Time: 3 minutes
Accessories/Prep: Fryer basket and 6 lightly sprayed silicone muffin cups

Serves 6

³⁄₄ cup all-purpose flour
¹⁄₂ teaspoon baking soda
¹⁄₄ cup granulated sugar
¹⁄₈ teaspoon salt
¹⁄₂ teaspoon vanilla extract
3 tablespoons unsalted
    butter, melted
2 large eggs
2 tablespoons whole milk
¹⁄₄ cup espresso baking chips

1 In a large bowl, combine flour, baking soda, sugar, and salt. In a separate medium bowl, combine vanilla, butter, eggs, and milk.

2 Pour wet ingredients from the medium bowl into the large bowl with dry ingredients. Gently combine ingredients. Fold in baking chips. Do not overmix. Divide mixture evenly among prepared silicone muffin cups.

3 Place muffin cups in fryer basket and bake 7 minutes. Transfer muffin cups to a cooling rack and let cool to room temperature. Serve warm.

PER MUFFIN

CALORIES: 221 | FAT: 10g | PROTEIN: 4g | SODIUM: 179mg | FIBER: 1g | CARBOHYDRATES: 26g | SUGAR: 13g

Cinnamon Cereal French Toast Sticks

Didn't use up that fresh loaf in time? Not to worry. Stale bread is the best vessel for French toast! Fresh bread can soak up your egg mixture too quickly and become soggy or limp. So consider that stale bread a sign that you deserve to make this delicious breakfast.

Hands-On Time: 10 minutes
Cook Time: 5 minutes
Preheat Temperature: 380°F
Preheat Time: 3 minutes
Accessories/Prep: Fryer basket lined with parchment paper

Serves 2

1 large egg
$\frac{1}{3}$ cup whole milk
$\frac{1}{8}$ teaspoon salt
1 cup crushed crunchy cinnamon breakfast cereal
4 slices hearty sandwich bread, each cut into 4 sticks
$\frac{1}{4}$ cup maple syrup

1 In a small bowl, whisk together egg, milk, and salt. Add crushed cereal to a second shallow bowl. Dip bread sticks in egg mixture. Dredge in cereal crumbs.

2 Place sticks in prepared fryer basket. Cook 3 minutes. Flip sticks. Cook an additional 2 minutes.

3 Transfer to a plate and serve warm with maple syrup to dip.

PER SERVING

CALORIES: 512 | FAT: 9g | PROTEIN: 13g | SODIUM: 785mg | FIBER: 7g | CARBOHYDRATES: 96g | SUGAR: 39g

Fried Chocolate, Hazelnut, and Banana Sandwiches

Of course this makes for a delicious breakfast sandwich for the kids, but adults can also indulge in this late-night treat! Crispy on the outside, melty on the inside—it doesn't get much better than this. (You can even have another one for dessert. Nobody has to know!)

Hands-On Time: 5 minutes
Cook Time: 12 minutes
Preheat Temperature: 350°F
Preheat Time: 3 minutes
Accessories/Prep: Fryer basket

Serves 2

3 tablespoons chocolate-hazelnut spread

4 slices hearty sandwich bread

1 large banana, peeled and sliced thin

2 tablespoons unsalted butter, melted

1 Spread chocolate-hazelnut spread on two slices of bread. Layer banana over chocolate-hazelnut spread. Top each with a second bread slice.

2 Brush the outside top and bottom of each sandwich lightly with melted butter.

3 Place one sandwich in fryer basket and cook 3 minutes. Flip and cook an additional 3 minutes. Repeat with remaining sandwich. Remove sandwiches to plates and serve warm.

PER SERVING

CALORIES: 498 | FAT: 21g | PROTEIN: 9g | SODIUM: 356mg | FIBER: 5g | CARBOHYDRATES: 67g | SUGAR: 27g

Pull-Apart Butter Biscuits

You can make these biscuits with runny eggs or a delicious jam, or smother them in a white sausage gravy.

Hands-On Time: 15 minutes
Cook Time: 9 minutes
Preheat Temperature: 350°F
Preheat Time: 3 minutes
Accessories/Prep: Fryer basket and greased pizza pan

Serves 4

2 cups self-rising flour, plus extra for flouring hands
½ teaspoon granulated sugar
4 tablespoons cold salted butter, cubed small
1 cup buttermilk

1 In a medium bowl using a fork or pastry cutter, combine flour, sugar, butter, and buttermilk until a sticky dough forms.

2 Flour your hands and form dough into eight balls. Place balls in prepared pizza pan. The biscuits will be touching. Place pizza pan in fryer basket and cook 9 minutes.

3 Transfer biscuits to a cooling rack. Let cool 5 minutes before pulling apart. Serve warm.

PER SERVING

CALORIES: 341 | **FAT:** 12g | **PROTEIN:** 6g | **SODIUM:** 765mg | **FIBER:** 1g | **CARBOHYDRATES:** 48g | **SUGAR:** 4g

Honey-Vanilla-Cinnamon–Baked Grapefruit

Grapefruit is an excellent source of antioxidants, making it a great way to start the day. The warmth of the honey, vanilla, and cinnamon will feel like a hug.

Hands-On Time: 5 minutes
Cook Time: 4 minutes
Preheat Temperature: 400°F
Preheat Time: 3 minutes
Accessories/Prep: Fryer basket

Serves 2

1 large grapefruit, halved
1 tablespoon honey
¼ teaspoon vanilla extract
¼ teaspoon ground cinnamon
⅛ teaspoon salt

1 Using a paring knife, cut each grapefruit section away from the inner membrane, leaving the sections in the fruit.

2 In a small bowl, combine honey, vanilla, cinnamon, and salt, and brush across grapefruit halves. Place in fryer basket. Cook 4 minutes.

3 Transfer grapefruit to bowls. Serve warm.

PER SERVING

CALORIES: 136 | **FAT:** 0g | **PROTEIN:** 2g | **SODIUM:** 145mg | **FIBER:** 4g | **CARBOHYDRATES:** 35g | **SUGAR:** 26g

Baked Peaches with Cottage Cheese

Cottage cheese pairs beautifully with peaches. But believe it or not, you can air fry fresh peach halves for an even tastier experience. The heat enhances the natural sugar in the fruit, making them even sweeter. Pair that with creamy cottage cheese and you've got yourself a delicious breakfast.

Hands-On Time: 5 minutes
Cook Time: 4 minutes
Preheat Temperature: 360°F
Preheat Time: 3 minutes
Accessories/Prep: Fryer basket

Serves 2

2 medium peaches, halved and pitted

¼ teaspoon ground cinnamon

4 teaspoons packed light brown sugar

1 cup full-fat cottage cheese

1 Evenly sprinkle the flat side of peach halves with cinnamon and brown sugar.

2 Place peaches skin side down in fryer basket. Cook 4 minutes.

3 Transfer peaches to plates and top with cottage cheese. Serve immediately.

PER SERVING

CALORIES: 203 | FAT: 3g | PROTEIN: 14g | SODIUM: 412mg | FIBER: 2g | CARBOHYDRATES: 27g | SUGAR: 25g

Homemade Granola

Forget the processed granola you find on the shelves of the grocery store, packed with sugar and preservatives. Keep control of what's in your breakfast cereal by making your own. This recipe is great with milk, over yogurt, or even as a topping for ice cream or frozen yogurt.

Hands-On Time: 10 minutes
Cook Time: 4 minutes
Preheat Temperature: 350°F
Preheat Time: 3 minutes
Accessories/Prep: Fryer basket and greased cake barrel

Serves 2

1 cup rolled oats
2 tablespoons sweetened coconut flakes
1 tablespoon pecan pieces
1 tablespoon raisins
1 tablespoon creamy peanut butter
1 tablespoon maple syrup
1 tablespoon packed light brown sugar
2 tablespoons unsalted butter, melted
¼ teaspoon salt

PERSONALIZE YOUR GRANOLA
Use this basic granola as a guide. You can mix it up by changing the nuts, adding seeds, using honey instead of maple syrup, or swapping out your raisins for dried cranberries. You can also add a little cinnamon or cocoa powder.

1 In a medium bowl, combine all ingredients. Place in prepared cake barrel.

2 Insert barrel in fryer basket and cook 2 minutes. Stir granola. Cook an additional 2 minutes.

3 Remove barrel from fryer basket and let cool completely. Serve immediately or store in an airtight container for up to 2 weeks.

PER SERVING

CALORIES: 413 | FAT: 21g | PROTEIN: 8g | SODIUM: 311mg | FIBER: 5g | CARBOHYDRATES: 50g | SUGAR: 20g

Spiced Apple Oatmeal Bake

There is just something about oatmeal on a cold winter's morning, especially with apples, raisins, and these warm spices. You can serve this recipe as is or with a dollop of yogurt. Even better, serve it after a meal with a scoop of ice cream for a comforting dessert.

Hands-On Time: 10 minutes
Cook Time: 8 minutes
Preheat Temperature: 325°F
Preheat Time: 3 minutes
Accessories/Prep: Fryer basket and greased cake barrel

Serves 4

1½ cups quick-cooking oats
⅓ cup packed light brown sugar
1 large egg
¼ cup whole milk
2 tablespoons unsalted butter, melted
1 medium Granny Smith apple, peeled, cored, and diced
¼ cup raisins
½ teaspoon ground cinnamon
¼ teaspoon ground nutmeg
⅛ teaspoon ground ginger
⅛ teaspoon salt

1 In a medium bowl, combine all ingredients. Transfer mixture to prepared cake barrel.

2 Place barrel in fryer basket and cook 8 minutes.

3 Transfer barrel to a cooling rack and allow to cool 5 minutes. Slice or scoop and serve warm.

PER SERVING

CALORIES: 310 | FAT: 9g | PROTEIN: 7g | SODIUM: 105mg | FIBER: 4g | CARBOHYDRATES: 52g | SUGAR: 28g

Fried SPAM, Egg, and Cheese Breakfast Sammies

A delicacy in Hawaii, SPAM is a brand of canned cooked pork. The air fryer not only crisps up the SPAM, but it evenly toasts the bread, making this a perfect sandwich for late nights.

Hands-On Time: 10 minutes
Cook Time: 11 minutes
Preheat Temperature: 375°F
Preheat Time: 3 minutes
Accessories/Prep: Fryer basket lined with parchment paper

Serves 4

1 (12-ounce) can SPAM, cut into 8 slices
8 slices sandwich bread
8 teaspoons mayonnaise
4 large eggs, scrambled
4 (³/₄-ounce) slices American cheese

1 Place SPAM slices in prepared fryer basket and cook 5 minutes. Flip slices. Cook an additional 5 minutes. Transfer to a plate.

2 While slices are cooking, spread each piece of bread with 1 teaspoon mayonnaise. Layer four bread slices with cooked eggs, cheese, and SPAM, and top with remaining bread slices, creating four sandwiches.

3 Place sandwiches in fryer basket and cook 1 minute. Serve warm.

PER SANDWICH

CALORIES: 634 | FAT: 39g | PROTEIN: 27g | SODIUM: 1,921mg | FIBER: 2g | CARBOHYDRATES: 40g | SUGAR: 9g

Molletes

The beans and pico de gallo in this open-faced sandwich really kick it up a notch!

Hands-On Time: 5 minutes
Cook Time: 7 minutes
Preheat Temperature: 375°F
Preheat Time: 3 minutes
Accessories/Prep: Fryer basket

Serves 4

2 bolillo rolls (or any crunchy bread), split lengthwise
1 cup refried beans
³/₄ cup shredded Monterey jack cheese
1 cup pico de gallo

1 Place rolls in fryer basket. Cook 5 minutes.

2 Top each roll with refried beans and cheese. Cook an additional 2 minutes.

3 Transfer open-faced sandwiches to plates and top with pico de gallo. Serve immediately.

PER MOLLETE

CALORIES: 238 | FAT: 7g | PROTEIN: 12g | SODIUM: 885mg | FIBER: 4g | CARBOHYDRATES: 31g | SUGAR: 6g

Huevos en Salsa de Tomate

Do you have a taste for spice? Enjoy a kick in your savory meals? Or does the thought of "hot" send you running for the hills? With this recipe, you're in control. Whatever kind of salsa you choose will impact the heat level. With the wide variety of salsas available, you're certain to find something to match your taste.

Hands-On Time: 10 minutes
Cook Time: 10 minutes
Preheat Temperature: 350°F
Preheat Time: 3 minutes
Accessories/Prep: Fryer basket and greased pizza pan

Serves 2

- 1/2 cup chunky salsa
- 2 large eggs
- 2 tablespoons crumbled cotija cheese
- 1 tablespoon chopped fresh cilantro
- 1/8 teaspoon salt

1 Spread salsa evenly in pizza pan. Place pan in fryer basket and cook 2 minutes.

2 Using the back of a spoon, form two holes in the salsa. Crack an egg in each hole. Sprinkle cotija around each egg. Cook an additional 8 minutes.

3 Remove pan from fryer basket. Garnish with cilantro and salt. Spoon into two bowls and serve warm.

PER SERVING

CALORIES: 114 | FAT: 6g | PROTEIN: 8g | SODIUM: 781mg | FIBER: 2g | CARBOHYDRATES: 5g | SUGAR: 4g

WHAT IS COTIJA CHEESE?

Crumbly like feta, cotija cheese is an aged (and deliciously addictive!) Mexican cheese named after the city. It is a semihard cheese now found in most grocery stores. Give it a try if you haven't already. If you can't find it, a Mexican blend of grated cheese is also delicious on this dish!

Chorizo Breakfast Sausage

Chorizo is a spicy Mexican pork sausage. Not only is it delicious in sauces, tacos, and meatballs, but it's wonderful with eggs for a kickin' breakfast. Although it can be purchased premade, knowing exactly what goes into your food is important. And making it is half the fun!

Hands-On Time: 10 minutes
Cook Time: 20 minutes
Preheat Temperature: 350°F
Preheat Time: 3 minutes
Accessories/Prep: Fryer basket; add 1 tablespoon water below basket

Serves 6

1 teaspoon smoked paprika
1 teaspoon dried oregano
1 teaspoon ground cumin
1 teaspoon chili powder
$1/4$ teaspoon cayenne pepper
$1/4$ teaspoon ground cinnamon
$1/2$ teaspoon salt
$1/2$ teaspoon ground black pepper
1 pound ground pork
2 medium cloves garlic, peeled and minced
2 tablespoons apple cider vinegar

1 In a large bowl, combine spices with a fork. Add ground pork, garlic, and vinegar and mix until combined. Form into twelve patties.

2 Place six patties in prepared fryer basket and cook 5 minutes. Flip patties. Cook an additional 5 minutes. Repeat with remaining patties.

3 Transfer to a plate and serve warm.

PER SERVING

CALORIES: 159 | FAT: 11g | PROTEIN: 14g | SODIUM: 252mg | FIBER: 1g | CARBOHYDRATES: 1g | SUGAR: 0g

Devilish Bacon and Eggs

Typically the first appetizer to disappear at the party, deviled eggs are a fan favorite. But they aren't only for backyard barbecues anymore. In a flash you can have these delectable bits ready (with a morning twist) with a recipe that's certain to please the whole family.

Hands-On Time: 5 minutes
Cook Time: 15 minutes
Preheat Temperature: 250°F
Preheat Time: 3 minutes
Accessories/Prep: Fryer basket and 4 lightly sprayed silicone muffin cups

Serves 4

4 large eggs
2 tablespoons mayonnaise
1 teaspoon yellow mustard
1 teaspoon pickle juice (from a jar of dill pickles)
$1/4$ teaspoon salt
$1/4$ teaspoon ground black pepper
2 slices bacon, cooked and quartered

WHY PICKLE JUICE?

Pickle juice adds a nice acidic hit to deviled eggs. White vinegar can be substituted, but most of us have a jar of pickles in the refrigerator, and the juice adds a little extra something. Sweet pickles will work as well as dill— whatever appeals to your taste.

1 Place each whole egg in a prepared muffin cup. Place cups in fryer basket and cook 15 minutes. While eggs are cooking, prepare a medium bowl of ice water. Transfer eggs immediately to ice water bath after cooking. Let sit 5 minutes, then peel eggs.

2 Slice eggs lengthwise, leaving whites intact, and set egg white halves aside. Transfer yolks to a medium bowl. Add mayonnaise, mustard, pickle juice, salt, and pepper to yolks. Using a fork, mash mixture until smooth.

3 Using either a spoon or a piping bag, divide yolk mixture evenly among egg white halves. Garnish each with a bacon piece and serve.

PER SERVING

CALORIES: 146 | FAT: 11g | PROTEIN: 8g | SODIUM: 388mg | FIBER: 0g | CARBOHYDRATES: 1g | SUGAR: 0g

Brekkie Flatbreads

Enjoy this hearty breakfast atop a crisp flatbread. The creaminess of the eggs, the fresh-ness of the peppery arugula, and the tartness of the goat cheese will have you coming back for this one again and again. Plus, it's almost like having pizza for breakfast!

Hands-On Time: 10 minutes
Cook Time: 8 minutes
Preheat Temperature: 375°F
Preheat Time: 3 minutes
Accessories/Prep: Fryer basket

Serves 2

2 (14-ounce) flatbreads

½ cup arugula

4 large eggs, scrambled and seasoned with ¼ teaspoon salt and ¼ teaspoon ground black pepper

½ cup crumbled goat cheese

2 teaspoons olive oil

2 teaspoons balsamic vinegar

1 Place one flatbread in fryer basket and cook 3 minutes.

2 Top toasted bread with half of scrambled eggs, ¼ cup arugula, and ¼ cup goat cheese. Cook 1 minute. Drizzle with 1 teaspoon oil and 1 teaspoon balsamic vinegar.

3 Repeat with second flatbread. Serve warm.

PER FLATBREAD

CALORIES: 1,561 | FAT: 53g | PROTEIN: 51g | SODIUM: 2,274mg | FIBER: 8g | CARBOHYDRATES: 208g | SUGAR: 17g

Short-Order Breakfast Quesadillas

This breakfast is perfect for a houseful of guests who wander into the kitchen at different times. Have all of the fixings ready, and let them choose what they like for a quick made-to-order morning delight! This dish tends to draw a crowd, so feel free to double (or triple!) the recipe.

Hands-On Time: 10 minutes
Cook Time: 16 minutes
Preheat Temperature: 350°F
Preheat Time: 3 minutes
Accessories/Prep: Fryer basket sprayed with olive oil cooking spray

Serves 4

½ pound bacon, cooked and crumbled
6 large eggs, scrambled
1 cup cubed cooked ham
2 medium Roma tomatoes, seeded and diced
1 medium avocado, peeled, pitted, and sliced
1 cup shredded Cheddar cheese
1 cup shredded Swiss cheese
8 (6") flour tortillas

1 Set out bacon crumbles, eggs, ham, tomatoes, avocado, and cheeses in separate dishes on the counter.

2 Place a tortilla in prepared fryer basket. Layer one-fourth of the bacon, scrambled eggs, ham, tomatoes, avocado, Cheddar, and Swiss evenly over tortilla. Top with second tortilla. Cook 4 minutes and transfer to a plate. Repeat with remaining tortillas.

3 Let cool 3 minutes. Slice and serve.

PER QUESADILLA

CALORIES: 707 | FAT: 39g | PROTEIN: 43g | SODIUM: 1,536mg | FIBER: 4g | CARBOHYDRATES: 38g | SUGAR: 4g

Italian Mozz and Egg Soufflés

Looking to impress guests? These soufflés will make a light and fluffy addition to your brunch table alongside fresh fruits and crispy bacon. Be sure to serve them immediately to take advantage of the airiness created in the air fryer!

Hands-On Time: 5 minutes
Cook Time: 12 minutes
Preheat Temperature: 280°F
Preheat Time: 3 minutes
Accessories/Prep: Fryer basket; 4 (6-ounce) ramekins sprayed with cooking spray

Serves 4

5 large eggs
2 tablespoons whole milk
1/4 cup shredded part-skim mozzarella cheese
1 medium Roma tomato, seeded and diced
1/4 teaspoon salt
1/4 teaspoon ground black pepper
1/4 teaspoon dried basil

1 In a medium bowl, whisk together eggs and milk. Stir in mozzarella, tomato, salt, pepper, and basil. Divide mixture evenly among prepared ramekins.

2 Place ramekins in fryer basket and cook 12 minutes.

3 Serve immediately while still fluffy.

PER SOUFFLÉ

CALORIES: 113 | FAT: 7g | PROTEIN: 10g | SODIUM: 274mg | FIBER: 0g | CARBOHYDRATES: 2g | SUGAR: 1g

Berry Delicious Toasted Bagels

You can bury your toaster in the appliance graveyard, because your air fryer can do this and more! Not only that, but it can do it *better*. Bagels that are crispy on top and bottom are the perfect vessel for a little cream cheese, and fresh berries take the dish to the next level.

Hands-On Time: 15 minutes
Cook Time: 4 minutes
Preheat Temperature: 370°F
Preheat Time: 3 minutes
Accessories/Prep: Fryer basket sprayed with olive oil cooking spray

Serves 2

2 plain bagels, halved
2 ounces cream cheese
1/3 cup blueberries
1/3 cup sliced strawberries
1 cinnamon graham cracker, crushed

1 Place split bagels cut side up in prepared fryer basket and cook 4 minutes.

2 Transfer bagels to plates. Spread each bagel half with 1 tablespoon cream cheese and top with berries.

3 Garnish with crushed graham cracker crumbs. Serve immediately.

PER BAGEL

CALORIES: 437 | FAT: 10g | PROTEIN: 14g | SODIUM: 695mg | FIBER: 4g | CARBOHYDRATES: 68g | SUGAR: 6g

Walnut Zucchini Bread

Zucchini not only lends a moistness to this bread, but it is also packed with vitamins A and C, along with fiber and potassium. With the addition of walnuts, the superfood list continues.

Hands-On Time: 10 minutes
Cook Time: 20 minutes
Preheat Temperature: 375°F
Preheat Time: 3 minutes
Accessories/Prep: Fryer basket; 7" springform pan sprayed with cooking spray

Serves 6

1 cup all-purpose flour
1/2 teaspoon baking soda
1/2 cup granulated sugar
1/4 teaspoon ground cinnamon
1/4 teaspoon salt
1/3 cup grated zucchini
1 large egg
1 tablespoon olive oil
1 teaspoon vanilla extract
1/4 cup chopped walnuts

1 In a medium bowl, combine all ingredients. Pour mixture into prepared springform pan.

2 Place pan in fryer basket and cook 20 minutes.

3 Remove pan from air fryer and let cool 10 minutes. Once cooled, remove springform sides. Slice and serve warm or at room temperature.

PER SERVING

CALORIES: 207 | FAT: 6g | PROTEIN: 4g | SODIUM: 214mg | FIBER: 1g | CARBOHYDRATES: 34g | SUGAR: 17g

Ham and Swiss Egg Cups

Eat these right out of the fryer, or make these easy egg cups the night before you'd like to eat them. Heat them up and go in the morning to avoid fast-food breakfast alternatives. You can also get creative with your stir-ins. A bacon and Cheddar egg cup would be a tasty variation!

Hands-On Time: 5 minutes
Cook Time: 8 minutes
Preheat Temperature: 350°F
Preheat Time: 3 minutes
Accessories/Prep: Fryer basket; 4 silicone muffin cups sprayed with cooking spray

Serves 4

4 large eggs
1 teaspoon yellow mustard
$1/4$ teaspoon salt
$1/4$ teaspoon ground black pepper
4 (2-ounce) slices deli ham, chopped
2 tablespoons shredded Swiss cheese

1 In a small bowl, whisk together eggs, mustard, salt, and pepper.

2 Divide whisked egg mixture evenly among prepared muffin cups. Evenly distribute ham and Swiss among cups.

3 Place muffin cups in fryer basket and cook 8 minutes. Transfer to a plate and serve warm. If you want them for the morning, refrigerate in an airtight container for up to 3 days. Microwave for approximately 20 seconds to reheat.

PER EGG CUP

CALORIES: 177 | FAT: 10g | PROTEIN: 17g | SODIUM: 880mg | FIBER: 1g | CARBOHYDRATES: 3g | SUGAR: 0g

3

Appetizers and Snacks

Gatherings of family and friends are fantastic. They are an integral part of our lives and our communities. But let's be honest: After cleaning the house, shopping for groceries, and getting yourself ready, you are probably exhausted. These air fryer appetizer and snack recipes take the pain out of laboring over the stove. With simplified directions, the prep time is reduced. In addition, you can cook in batches so that the hot appetizers are always flowing. Make a batch of margaritas and put your guests to work. After all, most of them like to help!

This chapter features amazing appetizers, from Charcuterie Board Fried Chickpeas and Italian Mozz Sticks with Marinara Dipping Sauce to Pesto Palmiers and Pepperoni Pizza Balls. Your guests will enjoy sampling all of these crispy creations. And when you are on your own, a quick snack of Reuben Pockets is where it's at!

Charcuterie Board Fried Chickpeas

These crispy little chickpeas will give your charcuterie board a boost! They are also delicious in salads or in a baggie in the car when you're on the go. Feel free to change up the dried spices when you need some variety.

Hands-On Time: 5 minutes
Cook Time: 16 minutes
Preheat Temperature: 350°F
Preheat Time: 3 minutes
Accessories/Prep: Fryer basket lined with aluminum foil

Serves 4

1 (15-ounce) can chickpeas, drained and rinsed
2 teaspoons olive oil
$1/2$ teaspoon salt
$1/4$ teaspoon ground black pepper

1 In a small bowl, toss chickpeas in oil. Place in prepared fryer basket.

2 Cook 5 minutes. Shake fryer basket, then cook an additional 5 minutes. Shake fryer basket again, and cook a final 6 minutes.

3 Transfer to a clean small bowl and toss with salt and pepper. Let cool and serve.

PER SERVING

CALORIES: 107 | FAT: 3g | PROTEIN: 4g | SODIUM: 425mg | FIBER: 4g | CARBOHYDRATES: 15g | SUGAR: 3g

Popcorn

You can make popcorn in your air fryer using less oil than you would in a saucepan. Simply drizzle melted butter on these kernels or go big and toss in some movie candy!

Hands-On Time: 5 minutes
Cook Time: 10 minutes
Preheat Temperature: 400°F
Preheat Time: 3 minutes
Accessories/Prep: Fryer basket

Serves 4

$1/3$ cup uncooked popcorn kernels
1 teaspoon olive oil
$1/2$ teaspoon salt

1 In a small bowl, toss popcorn kernels in oil. Place in fryer basket.

2 Cook 10 minutes or until kernels stop popping.

3 Transfer to a medium bowl and toss with salt. Serve warm.

PER SERVING

CALORIES: 91 | FAT: 2g | PROTEIN: 3g | SODIUM: 292mg | FIBER: 3g | CARBOHYDRATES: 16g | SUGAR: 0g

Buttered Chex Snack

Hello, the 1970s called! Are you wearing your flared pants? Have you pulled up your tube socks? Well, then you are in the right place. Butter your Chex and enjoy this way-back snack! Feelings of nostalgia guaranteed.

Hands-On Time: 5 minutes
Cook Time: 6 minutes
Preheat Temperature: 370°F
Preheat Time: 3 minutes
Accessories/Prep: Fryer basket

Serves 4

3 cups Corn Chex cereal
2 tablespoons unsalted butter, melted
1/4 teaspoon salt

1 In a large bowl, toss cereal in melted butter. Place in fryer basket.

2 Cook 3 minutes. Shake fryer basket, then cook an additional 3 minutes.

3 Transfer to a clean bowl and toss with salt. Serve warm or at room temperature.

PER SERVING

CALORIES: 136 | FAT: 6g | PROTEIN: 2g | SODIUM: 322mg | FIBER: 1g | CARBOHYDRATES: 20g | SUGAR: 3g

Everything Pumpkin Seeds

After you gut those beautiful pumpkins to carve in autumn, remember to save the seeds! You can toast them up for a tasty and healthy snack. This recipe calls for olive oil, but if you can get your hands on some pumpkin oil, well, why not?

Hands-On Time: 10 minutes
Cook Time: 15 minutes
Preheat Temperature: 350°F
Preheat Time: 3 minutes
Accessories/Prep: Fryer basket

Serves 6

2 cups fresh pumpkin seeds
2 tablespoons olive oil
1/2 teaspoon salt
2 tablespoons everything bagel seasoning

1 In a medium bowl, combine all ingredients. Place in fryer basket.

2 Cook 15 minutes, tossing every 5 minutes. Transfer seeds to a bowl and let cool to room temperature.

3 Serve immediately or store in an airtight container in the pantry for up to 2 weeks.

PER SERVING

CALORIES: 285 | FAT: 22g | PROTEIN: 12g | SODIUM: 520mg | FIBER: 3g | CARBOHYDRATES: 6g | SUGAR: 1g

Italian Mozz Sticks with Marinara Dipping Sauce

Mozzarella sticks are sometimes thought of as bar food. But you don't have to go to happy hour for these ooey-gooey mozz sticks. Instead, invite your friends over, crack a bottle, and let your air fryer do the work! These will satisfy your cravings and are certain to be a crowd-pleaser.

Hands-On Time: 15 minutes
Cook Time: 20 minutes
Preheat Temperature: 400°F
Preheat Time: 3 minutes
Accessories/Prep: Fryer basket lined with parchment paper

Serves 6

2 tablespoons all-purpose flour
1 large egg
1 tablespoon whole milk
½ cup Italian-style bread crumbs
¼ teaspoon salt
12 (1-ounce) mozzarella cheese sticks (string cheese)
2 teaspoons olive oil, divided
½ cup marinara sauce, warmed

1   Place flour in a small bowl. In a separate small bowl, whisk together egg and milk. In a third small bowl, combine bread crumbs and salt.

2   Dredge 1 mozzarella stick in flour. Shake off excess flour, then dip in egg mixture. Shake off excess egg and dredge in bread crumb mixture. Shake off excess bread crumbs. Transfer to a plate and repeat with remaining mozzarella sticks. Place in freezer 10 minutes.

3   Place 6 sticks in prepared fryer basket. Brush with ½ teaspoon oil. Cook 3 minutes. Gently flip mozzarella and brush with remaining oil. Cook an additional 2 minutes. Transfer to a serving dish and repeat with remaining mozzarella sticks. Serve warm with marinara sauce for dipping.

PER SERVING

CALORIES: 283 | FAT: 18g | PROTEIN: 18g | SODIUM: 766mg | FIBER: 1g | CARBOHYDRATES: 11g | SUGAR: 2g

Bacon-Wrapped Blue Cheese–Stuffed Dates

This recipe features a glorious combination. The sweet dates, ripe blue cheese, and salty bacon are something special together. Adding the acidity of a simple marinara takes these bites to the next level.

Hands-On Time: 15 minutes
Cook Time: 12 minutes
Preheat Temperature: 350°F
Preheat Time: 3 minutes
Accessories/Prep: Fryer basket with 2 tablespoons water below basket

Serves 6

- 1/2 cup crumbled blue cheese
- 12 medium Medjool dates, pitted
- 6 slices uncooked bacon, halved
- 1/2 cup marinara sauce, warmed

1 Press about 2 teaspoons blue cheese into each date. Wrap each date with half a slice bacon.

2 Place wrapped dates in prepared fryer basket. Cook 12 minutes.

3 Transfer dates to a plate and let cool 10 minutes. Serve warm with marinara sauce for dipping.

PER SERVING

CALORIES: 226 | FAT: 6g | PROTEIN: 7g | SODIUM: 383mg | FIBER: 4g | CARBOHYDRATES: 38g | SUGAR: 33g

Roasted Red Peppers

Roasted Red Peppers can be used on pizzas, in salads, in casseroles, and even blended into sauces. Removing the skin is key, so don't skip the step of letting them cool in a bowl topped with plastic wrap. These peppers will bring flavor to most any dish. You're limited only by your imagination!

Hands-On Time: 5 minutes
Cook Time: 20 minutes
Preheat Temperature: 370°F
Preheat Time: 3 minutes
Accessories/Prep: Fryer basket

Serves 4

2 medium red bell peppers, halved and seeded

ROASTED RED PEPPER SAUCE

This sauce is perfect mixed into pasta, on a fancy flatbread, or as an accompaniment to any charcuterie board. Using a blender or food processor, simply blend or pulse the following until smooth: Roasted Red Peppers from this recipe, ⅓ cup olive oil, ¼ cup chopped pecans, ¼ cup heavy cream, 1 medium clove garlic (minced), 1 tablespoon lemon juice, ½ teaspoon salt, and ¼ cup chopped fresh basil. Taste. Add salt if necessary.

1 Place bell peppers cut side up in fryer basket. Cook 10 minutes. Flip pepper halves and cook an additional 10 minutes.

2 Transfer peppers to a medium bowl and cover with plastic wrap. Let cool completely. This will help steam the skins loose.

3 Remove skins. Transfer to an airtight container and refrigerate covered up to 4 days.

PER SERVING

CALORIES: 18 | FAT: 0g | PROTEIN: 1g | SODIUM: 2mg | FIBER: 1g | CARBOHYDRATES: 4g | SUGAR: 3g

Pimiento Cheese–Stuffed Mini Sweet Peppers

This classic southern spread of cheese, mayonnaise, and pimientos is traditionally served in a sandwich or with crackers, but it makes the perfect filling for mini peppers. If you like things with a little kick, look for jalapeño pimiento cheese!

Hands-On Time: 10 minutes
Cook Time: 8 minutes
Preheat Temperature: 350°F
Preheat Time: 3 minutes
Accessories/Prep: Fryer basket

Serves 4

- ½ cup pimiento cheese spread
- 8 mini sweet bell peppers, halved lengthwise and seeded

HOMEMADE PIMIENTO CHEESE SPREAD

Although prepared pimiento cheese spread can be purchased in the deli section of most grocery stores, making it couldn't be any easier! Just combine 16 ounces finely shredded Cheddar cheese with 1 (4-ounce) jar pimientos including juice, ½ cup mayonnaise, ¼ teaspoon salt, and ¼ teaspoon ground black pepper. Refrigerate covered for up to 10 days.

1 Press about ½ tablespoon pimiento cheese into each pepper half.

2 Place peppers in fryer basket and cook 8 minutes.

3 Transfer to a plate and serve warm.

PER SERVING

CALORIES: 76 | FAT: 7g | PROTEIN: 4g | SODIUM: 285mg | FIBER: 1g | CARBOHYDRATES: 7g | SUGAR: 5g

Smoky Onion Rings

Onion rings are excellent as a side for burgers or steaks, or on their own as a snack. But sometimes we forego this deep-fried treat due to the fat content. Enter the air fryer. By reducing the fat considerably, you can once again give these circular delights a place at the table!

Hands-On Time: 10 minutes
Cook Time: 21 minutes
Preheat Temperature: 400°F
Preheat Time: 3 minutes
Accessories/Prep: Fryer basket

Serves 2

1 cup all-purpose flour
$1/4$ cup cornstarch
2 large eggs
1 tablespoon water
1 tablespoon sriracha
1 cup panko bread crumbs
1 teaspoon smoked paprika
$1/2$ teaspoon salt
1 large sweet onion, peeled, trimmed, and sliced into $1/4$" rounds

1 In a small bowl, combine flour and corn-starch. In a separate small bowl, whisk together eggs, water, and sriracha. In a third small bowl, combine bread crumbs, paprika, and salt.

2 Separate onion slices into individual rings. Dredge a ring in flour mixture. Shake off excess flour, then dip in egg mixture. Shake off excess egg and dredge in bread crumbs. Shake off excess bread crumbs. Transfer to a plate and repeat with remaining onion rings.

3 Working in batches as necessary, place coated onion rings in fryer basket. Cook 7 minutes or until crispy. Transfer to a plate and repeat with remaining onion rings. Serve warm.

PER SERVING

CALORIES: 276 | FAT: 3g | PROTEIN: 9g | SODIUM: 459mg | FIBER: 2g | CARBOHYDRATES: 51g | SUGAR: 5g

Ranch Potato Chips

Slicing the potato into consistent paper-thin slices is the key to perfect potato chips. A mandoline is a worthy purchase to help achieve this. The air fryer will brown the edges, but be sure to keep checking the chips toward the end of the cooking time. They can go from brown to burned quickly!

Hands-On Time: 10 minutes
Cook Time: 47 minutes
Preheat Temperature: 400°F
Preheat Time: 3 minutes
Accessories/Prep: Fryer basket

Serves 2

- 1 medium russet potato, sliced into $1/8$" rounds
- 2 teaspoons olive oil
- 2 teaspoons dry ranch seasoning mix, divided

1 Soak potato slices in room temperature water 30 minutes. Drain and dry completely by patting with paper towels.

2 In a medium bowl, combine potato slices, oil, and 1 teaspoon seasoning. Toss to coat. Place potato slices in fryer basket and cook 6 minutes. Shake fryer basket, then cook an additional 5 minutes. Shake fryer basket again and cook a final 6 minutes.

3 Transfer to a clean bowl and toss chips with remaining seasoning. Let rest 15 minutes. Serve.

PER SERVING

CALORIES: 125 | FAT: 4g | PROTEIN: 2g | SODIUM: 274mg | FIBER: 1g | CARBOHYDRATES: 19g | SUGAR: 1g

Tortilla Chips

If you are tired of just eating off the vegetable tray on football Sunday, make your own tortilla chips and cut out the deep-fried grease! These guilt-free yet crispy Tortilla Chips couldn't be easier or tastier—especially when paired with a fresh Pico Guacamole.

Hands-On Time: 5 minutes
Cook Time: 15 minutes
Preheat Temperature: 400°F
Preheat Time: 3 minutes
Accessories/Prep: Fryer basket

Serves 4

6 (6") corn tortillas, each cut into 6 triangles
Olive oil cooking spray
$1/2$ teaspoon salt, divided

TRY A BATCH OF PICO GUACAMOLE

In this fresh, delicious dip, tomatoes are a welcome addition to a traditional guacamole. To make it, combine the following in a small bowl: 1 tablespoon fresh lime juice; 2 medium peeled, pitted, and mashed avocados; 4 medium peeled and minced cloves garlic; 1 teaspoon sriracha; 1 teaspoon salt; $1/4$ cup chopped fresh cilantro; and 2 seeded and diced medium Roma tomatoes. Refrigerate covered for up to 3 days.

1 Spray tortilla triangles with cooking spray. Sprinkle with $1/4$ teaspoon salt.

2 Place one-third of chips in fryer basket. Cook 3 minutes. Flip chips. Cook 2 minutes. Transfer chips from fryer basket to a baking sheet so they can be spread out. Season with salt, reserving enough salt for remaining chips. When cooled, add chips to a large bowl. Repeat with remaining two batches.

3 Let all chips cool 5 minutes. Serve.

PER SERVING

CALORIES: 78 | FAT: 1g | PROTEIN: 2g | SODIUM: 306mg | FIBER: 2g | CARBOHYDRATES: 16g | SUGAR: 0g

Cornmeal-Crusted Fried Green Tomatoes

Fried green tomatoes are about as southern as biscuits and gravy! This simple dish is a perfect treat in summer, when tomatoes are in peak season. Pair them with your favorite dipping sauce, or try them in the Fried Green Tomato BLTs recipe in this chapter for a delicious twist on an all-time favorite.

Hands-On Time: 15 minutes
Cook Time: 9 minutes
Preheat Temperature: 400°F
Preheat Time: 3 minutes
Accessories/Prep: Fryer basket lined with aluminum foil

Serves 4

⅓ cup all-purpose flour
¼ cup whole buttermilk
⅓ cup yellow cornmeal
1 teaspoon salt
2 large green tomatoes, trimmed and sliced into ½" rounds
1 tablespoon olive oil

COMEBACK SAUCE

A little sweet, a little spicy, this southern sauce will have you coming back for more. Combine these in a small bowl: ½ cup mayonnaise, 2 tablespoons honey, 2 tablespoons ketchup, ½ teaspoon Worcestershire sauce, ½ teaspoon Dijon mustard, ½ teaspoon sriracha, 1 medium clove garlic (peeled and minced), ¼ teaspoon smoked paprika, ¼ teaspoon salt, and ¼ teaspoon ground black pepper. Refrigerate covered for up to 3 days.

1   Place flour and buttermilk in two separate shallow bowls. In a third shallow bowl, combine cornmeal and salt.

2   Dredge 1 tomato slice in flour. Shake off excess flour, then dip in buttermilk. Shake off excess buttermilk and dredge in cornmeal mixture. Shake off excess cornmeal. Transfer to a plate and repeat with remaining tomato slices. Place slices in prepared fryer basket. Lightly brush the top of each tomato slice with oil.

3   Cook 5 minutes. Flip tomato slices and lightly brush again with oil. Cook 4 minutes. Transfer tomato slices to a plate and serve warm.

PER SERVING

CALORIES: 134 | FAT: 4g | PROTEIN: 3g | SODIUM: 612mg | FIBER: 2g | CARBOHYDRATES: 21g | SUGAR: 4g

Crispy Croutons

Day-old bread works best for these little delights. This recipe calls for a baguette, but most hearty artisanal breads will work perfectly. Also, different bread varieties will yield different croutons. The same goes for the herb used. Try swapping out the basil for oregano, thyme, or a mix of Italian seasonings!

Hands-On Time: 10 minutes
Cook Time: 6 minutes
Preheat Temperature: 380°F
Preheat Time: 3 minutes
Accessories/Prep: Fryer basket

Serves 4

2 tablespoons olive oil
$1/4$ teaspoon dried basil
$1/2$ teaspoon garlic powder
$1/4$ teaspoon salt
20 ($3/4$") cubes cut from a French baguette

1 In a medium bowl, whisk together oil, basil, garlic powder, and salt. Add bread cubes and toss to coat.

2 Place bread cubes in fryer basket and cook 3 minutes. Shake fryer basket, then cook an additional 3 minutes.

3 Transfer croutons to a basket. Serve immediately or let cool completely and store in an airtight container in the pantry for up to 1 week.

PER SERVING

CALORIES: 176 | FAT: 7g | PROTEIN: 5g | SODIUM: 401mg | FIBER: 1g | CARBOHYDRATES: 22g | SUGAR: 2g

Fried Green Tomato BLTs

It's time to bring your BLT to the next level. Instead of that garden-fresh tomato slice, try a fried green tomato. The result is the same fresh taste with an extra crunch!

Hands-On Time: 10 minutes
Cook Time: 3 minutes
Preheat Temperature: 350°F
Preheat Time: 3 minutes
Accessories/Prep: Fryer basket lined with aluminum foil

Serves 2

4 slices sandwich bread
2 tablespoons unsalted butter, melted
$1/4$ cup mayonnaise
6 slices Cornmeal-Crusted Fried Green Tomatoes (see recipe in this chapter)
6 slices cooked bacon
6 butter lettuce leaves

1 Brush one side of each piece of bread with melted butter. Place bread butter side up in prepared fryer basket. Cook 3 minutes.

2 Remove bread from fryer basket. Spread mayonnaise on unbuttered sides of bread. On 2 bread slices, layer 3 tomato slices, 3 slices bacon, and 3 lettuce leaves. Top with remaining slices of bread to form two sandwiches.

3 Serve warm.

PER SANDWICH

CALORIES: 781 | FAT: 48g | PROTEIN: 22g | SODIUM: 1,875mg | FIBER: 5g | CARBOHYDRATES: 62g | SUGAR: 11g

Pesto Palmiers

Need an excuse to use up your jar of pesto? Savory or sweet, palmiers elevate whatever you choose to spread on them before rolling them up into crisp slices. Pesto turns them into a mouthwatering snack that's both crispy and luxurious.

Hands-On Time: 15 minutes
Cook Time: 54 minutes
Preheat Temperature: 350°F
Preheat Time: 3 minutes
Accessories/Prep: Fryer basket lined with parchment paper

Serves 6

2 teaspoons all-purpose flour
1 sheet thawed frozen phyllo dough, room temperature
1 tablespoon unsalted butter, melted
¼ cup pesto

HOMEMADE PESTO

Although many different flavors of prepared pesto are available, you can also make your own and take advantage of your herb garden! In a food processor, pulse ¾ cup fresh basil leaves, ½ cup fresh chopped parsley, 4 peeled medium cloves garlic, ¼ cup pine nuts, ⅓ cup shredded Parmesan cheese, ¼ teaspoon salt, and ⅛ teaspoon ground black pepper. While the processor is running, slowly drizzle ¼ cup oil into mixture until emulsified. Taste and add additional salt if necessary.

1 Sprinkle flour over a flat, clean work surface. Lay phyllo dough on work surface and brush with butter. Spread pesto evenly over dough. Starting at the long end carefully roll one end toward the middle of sheet. Stop at the halfway point. Roll opposite side toward the middle. Refrigerate 30 minutes.

2 Slice log into eighteen equal slices. Place six palmiers in prepared fryer basket. Cook 8 minutes, then transfer to a cooling rack. Repeat with remaining palmiers.

3 Serve warm or at room temperature.

PER SERVING

CALORIES: 62 | FAT: 5g | PROTEIN: 1g | SODIUM: 115mg | FIBER: 0g | CARBOHYDRATES: 3g | SUGAR: 0g

Cheesy Croutons for Soup

If you like fresh croutons floating on top of a creamy bowl of tomato-basil soup, then you'll love these grilled cheese croutons. An unexpected pop of cheese is always welcome. Try out different cheeses with different soups for a new experience each time. Pssst...feta croutons are amazing on a fresh Greek salad!

Hands-On Time: 10 minutes
Cook Time: 12 minutes
Preheat Temperature: 350°F
Preheat Time: 3 minutes
Accessories/Prep: Fryer basket

Serves 4

- 4 slices hearty sandwich bread
- 2 ($3/4$-ounce) slices American cheese
- 2 ($2/3$-ounce) slices provolone cheese
- 2 tablespoons unsalted butter, melted

1. Form a sandwich by layering 1 slice of bread, 1 slice of American cheese, 1 slice of provolone, and another slice of bread. Repeat to make a second sandwich.

2. Brush the top and bottom of each sandwich lightly with melted butter. Place in fryer basket one at a time and cook 3 minutes. Transfer sandwich to a clean flat surface. Gently press sandwich flat with a heavy flat pan or skillet. Return flattened sandwich to fryer basket and cook 3 minutes. Repeat with second sandwich.

3. Cut sandwiches into 1" cubes and float in preferred bowl of soup or use as a salad topping.

PER SERVING

CALORIES: 206 | FAT: 10g | PROTEIN: 8g | SODIUM: 408mg | FIBER: 1g | CARBOHYDRATES: 19g | SUGAR: 3g

Greek Puff Rolls

When you're craving Mediterranean flavors, nothing else will satisfy. These delicious rolls are a perfect appetizer to share with friends or family, and although they're a breeze to whip up, they seem like a fancy snack. Fellow snackers will be begging for the recipe!

Hands-On Time: 15 minutes
Cook Time: 42 minutes
Preheat Temperature: 350°F
Preheat Time: 3 minutes
Accessories/Prep: Fryer basket lined with parchment paper

Serves 5

- 1 tablespoon all-purpose flour
- 1 sheet thawed frozen phyllo dough, room temperature
- 1 tablespoon unsalted butter, melted
- 2 tablespoons crumbled feta cheese
- 2 tablespoons minced kalamata olives
- 1 teaspoon garlic salt

1 Sprinkle flour on a clean work surface. Place phyllo sheet on floured work surface and brush butter over phyllo. Evenly scatter feta, olives, and garlic salt over phyllo sheet. Starting at a short end, roll into a log. Refrigerate 30 minutes.

2 Slice log into ten equal slices.

3 Place five slices in prepared fryer basket. Cook 6 minutes. Transfer to a cooling rack. Repeat with remaining slices. Serve warm.

PER SERVING

CALORIES: 60 | FAT: 5g | PROTEIN: 1g | SODIUM: 536mg | FIBER: 0g | CARBOHYDRATES: 3g | SUGAR: 0g

Crispy Wontons

This is likely one of those dishes you never imagined you could make at home before the air fryer came into your life! Whether you serve these next to fried rice or float them in a pho broth, these crispy wontons are certain to take your dish up a notch.

Hands-On Time: 30 minutes
Cook Time: 24 minutes
Preheat Temperature: 330°F
Preheat Time: 3 minutes
Accessories/Prep: Fryer basket sprayed with cooking spray

Serves 6

1 cup bagged angel-hair coleslaw mix
2 medium scallions, trimmed and finely chopped (green and white parts included)
1 large carrot, peeled and grated
1 tablespoon finely diced fresh ginger
3 medium cloves garlic, peeled and minced
1 teaspoon soy sauce
1 teaspoon rice vinegar
$1/2$ teaspoon sriracha
30 wonton wrappers
Olive oil cooking spray

1 In a large bowl, combine coleslaw, scallions, carrot, ginger, garlic, soy sauce, vinegar, and sriracha.

2 Place 1 wonton wrapper on a cutting board. Place 1 teaspoon coleslaw mixture in the center of wrapper. Dip your finger in water and run it around the perimeter of the wonton. Fold one corner over to meet the opposite corner, forming a triangle. Press edges to seal. Repeat with remaining wontons and filling.

3 Place ten wontons in prepared fryer basket. Spray tops with cooking spray. Cook 8 minutes. Transfer wontons to a plate. Repeat with remaining wontons. Serve warm.

PER SERVING

CALORIES: 129 | FAT: 0g | PROTEIN: 4g | SODIUM: 296mg | FIBER: 2g | CARBOHYDRATES: 26g | SUGAR: 1g

Sweet Hawaiian Ham and Swiss Pockets

Although plain crescent rolls can be used in this recipe, the sweet Hawaiian flavor marries nicely with the savory ham and Swiss combination. And the tangy, sharp flavor of the Dijon mustard pulls everything together in perfect balance.

Hands-On Time: 15 minutes
Cook Time: 7 minutes
Preheat Temperature: 350°F
Preheat Time: 3 minutes
Accessories/Prep: Fryer basket sprayed with cooking spray

Serves 4

1 (8-ounce) tube refrigerated Hawaiian crescent rolls
4 teaspoons Dijon mustard
4 ounces deli ham, sliced into 4 pieces
4 tablespoons shredded Swiss cheese

TAKE A HIKE!

If you are planning on hitting the trails, whip up a batch of these pocket sandwiches. They are portable, light, and can fit easily in your backpack. Also, don't be afraid to get creative with the variety of meats and cheeses available.

1 Open tube of crescent rolls and lay out dough on a cutting board. Cut into four equal rectangles and pinch dough together where separated.

2 On one half of each rectangle, spread 1 teaspoon Dijon mustard. Add 1 slice of ham and 1 tablespoon Swiss. Fold over into a small rectangle and use a fork to seal the edges.

3 Place pockets in prepared fryer basket. Cook 7 minutes. Remove, let cool 5 minutes, and serve warm.

PER POCKET

CALORIES: 283 | FAT: 14g | PROTEIN: 11g | SODIUM: 878mg | FIBER: 0g | CARBOHYDRATES: 26g | SUGAR: 6g

Reuben Pockets

Reubens contain one of the best flavor combinations in the deli world. It's so good, it shouldn't need to be confined to sandwiches! For the same flavor profile on the go, try this version with crescent rolls.

Hands-On Time: 15 minutes
Cook Time: 7 minutes
Preheat Temperature: 350°F
Preheat Time: 3 minutes
Accessories/Prep: Fryer basket sprayed with cooking spray

Serves 4

1 (8-ounce) tube refrigerated crescent rolls
4 teaspoons Thousand Island salad dressing
4 (1-ounce) slices pastrami
4 tablespoons shredded Swiss cheese
4 tablespoons drained sauerkraut
4 teaspoons caraway seeds

1 Open tube of crescent rolls and lay out dough on a cutting board. Cut into four equal rectangles and pinch dough together where separated.

2 On one half of each rectangle, spread 1 teaspoon dressing. Layer 1 slice pastrami, 1 tablespoon Swiss, and 1 tablespoon sauerkraut on top of dressing. Fold the other side of the rectangle over and use a fork to seal the edges. Press 1 teaspoon caraway seeds into the top of each pocket.

3 Place pockets in prepared fryer basket. Cook 7 minutes. Remove, let cool 5 minutes, and serve warm.

PER POCKET

CALORIES: 282 | FAT: 14g | PROTEIN: 12g | SODIUM: 824mg | FIBER: 1g | CARBOHYDRATES: 27g | SUGAR: 7g

Pepperoni Pizza Balls

After-school treats have never been easier—or tastier! With just four ingredients, 30 minutes, and an air fryer, you can whip up this delicious snack. They may even be better than ordering a pie for takeout. After all, who doesn't like pizza—no matter what form it takes!

Hands-On Time: 15 minutes
Cook Time: 15 minutes
Preheat Temperature: 320°F
Preheat Time: 3 minutes
Accessories/Prep: Fryer basket lined with parchment paper

Serves 8

1 (16.3-ounce) can refrigerated oversized biscuits (8 total)
2 cups pizza sauce, divided
1 cup shredded part-skim mozzarella cheese
16 slices pepperoni

1 Open can of biscuits and separate on a cutting board. Roll out each biscuit into a circle about ¼" thick.

2 In the center of each biscuit circle, spread 2 tablespoons pizza sauce. Layer 2 tablespoons mozzarella and 2 slices pepperoni on top of sauce. Fold dough up to a point and pinch to seal. Place in prepared fryer basket seam side down.

3 Cook 15 minutes. Transfer to a cooling rack and let rest 5 minutes. Warm remaining pizza sauce for dipping. Serve warm with sauce.

PER PIZZA BALL

CALORIES: 273 | FAT: 10g | PROTEIN: 9g | SODIUM: 941mg | FIBER: 3g | CARBOHYDRATES: 35g | SUGAR: 7g

Pork and Boursin-Stuffed Mushrooms

This is one of those easy-to-assemble appetizers that you'll have to double (or triple!) because your guests will keep coming back for more. And don't tell anyone, but they are super easy to prepare, and you can air fry them on demand so that they are warm and ready to go whenever!

Hands-On Time: 10 minutes
Cook Time: 6 minutes
Preheat Temperature: 350°F
Preheat Time: 3 minutes
Accessories/Prep: Fryer basket

Serves 2

1 teaspoon olive oil
12 whole white button mushroom caps, stems removed
1/4 pound pork sausage, cooked
1 tablespoon grated yellow onion
1/4 cup Boursin cheese (Garlic & Fine Herbs flavor)
2 tablespoons panko bread crumbs

1 Brush oil over top ridge of each mushroom cap.

2 In a small bowl, combine sausage, onion, and Boursin. Divide evenly and press mixture into mushroom caps. Sprinkle bread crumbs evenly on top.

3 Place stuffed mushrooms in fryer basket. Cook 6 minutes. Transfer to a plate and serve warm.

PER SERVING

CALORIES: 286 | FAT: 23g | PROTEIN: 15g | SODIUM: 501mg | FIBER: 1g | CARBOHYDRATES: 5g | SUGAR: 3g

WHAT IS BOURSIN CHEESE?
Boursin cheese has the consistency of cream cheese and is a product of Normandy. The magic of Boursin is that it has already been seasoned for you. Boursin can be found with the specialty cheeses in the deli section of most grocers. It comes in a variety of flavors and can be used as a spread or in recipes such as this.

4

Side Dishes

Side dishes aren't typically the center of attention, but in some cases they can be the best part of a meal—particularly if they're made from a recipe in this chapter. An entrée just isn't the same without them.

We all know side dishes are meant to be a complement to main dishes; however, oftentimes those healthy and nutritional options in the sides get haphazardly thrown together or nixed altogether because of our hectic lives. Thankfully, the air fryer does all the heavy lifting for you so you can quickly roast vegetables and cook other sides while you put your attention on the main course.

Whether you need some Shoestring French Fries with your burger, some Blistered Tomatoes with your baked halibut, or some Buttered Corn on the Cob with your grilled chicken, this chapter has got you covered. Simplified recipes make it easy to make these sides, and your body and taste buds will thank you!

Buttered Corn on the Cob

Corn on the cob can easily be cooked in the air fryer, freeing up the stove for the rest of the meal. Here's a shucking hack: Use a toothbrush to quickly pull out those strands!

Hands-On Time: 5 minutes
Cook Time: 8 minutes
Preheat Temperature: 380°F
Preheat Time: 3 minutes
Accessories/Prep: Fryer basket

Serves 4

4 ears corn, shucked
3 tablespoons unsalted
   butter, melted, divided
1/2 teaspoon salt

1 Place corn in fryer basket and brush with half the butter.

2 Cook 8 minutes.

3 Transfer corn to a plate and brush with remaining butter. Season with salt. Serve warm.

PER EAR OF CORN

CALORIES: 163 | FAT: 9g | PROTEIN: 3g | SODIUM: 306mg | FIBER: 2g | CARBOHYDRATES: 19g | SUGAR: 6g

Simple Roasted Garlic

Garlic, once roasted, becomes butterlike. Spread it on baguette slices, add it to mashed potatoes, combine it with mayonnaise for an awesome aioli for burgers, or spread it atop a steak in the last few minutes of grilling.

Hands-On Time: 10 minutes
Cook Time: 45 minutes
Preheat Temperature: 350°F
Preheat Time: 3 minutes
Accessories/Prep: Fryer basket

Serves 4

4 teaspoons olive oil
2 whole bulbs garlic, unpeeled,
   1/4" trimmed from top
1/8 teaspoon salt

1 Drizzle oil over garlic bulbs and rub it in with your fingers. Season bulbs with salt.

2 Roll each bulb up in a square of aluminum foil. Place wrapped bulbs in ungreased fryer basket. Cook 45 minutes.

3 Unwrap each bulb and allow to sit until cool enough to handle. When cooled, squeeze roasted garlic cloves from garlic skins. Store unused cloves refrigerated in an airtight container for up to 3 days.

PER TABLESPOON

CALORIES: 66 | FAT: 4g | PROTEIN: 1g | SODIUM: 75mg | FIBER: 0g | CARBOHYDRATES: 6g | SUGAR: 0g

Roasted Red Pepper and Jack Corn Bread

Corn bread is a southern staple, but add just two crucial ingredients, red peppers and Monterey jack cheese, and you've transformed this side into an entirely new, flavor-packed bread! Try a square served with a slice of ham or even alongside a burrito bowl. The opportunities are truly endless.

Hands-On Time: 10 minutes
Cook Time: 15 minutes
Preheat Temperature: 350°F
Preheat Time: 3 minutes
Accessories/Prep: Fryer basket; pizza pan sprayed with cooking spray

Serves 4

1 large egg, whisked
1 cup self-rising buttermilk cornmeal mix
1/2 cup shredded Monterey jack cheese
1/4 cup drained jarred diced roasted red peppers
1/2 cup whole buttermilk
1/2 teaspoon granulated sugar
1/8 teaspoon salt
1/8 teaspoon ground black pepper

1 In a large bowl, combine egg, cornmeal mix, Monterey jack, red peppers, buttermilk, sugar, salt, and black pepper. Do not overmix.

2 Transfer mixture to prepared pizza pan, then place pan in fryer basket. Cook 15 minutes or until an inserted toothpick comes out clean. Transfer pan to a cooling rack. Let rest 5 minutes.

3 Flip onto a plate and slice corn bread. Serve warm.

PER SERVING

CALORIES: 196 | **FAT:** 7g | **PROTEIN:** 9g | **SODIUM:** 660mg | **FIBER:** 2g | **CARBOHYDRATES:** 24g | **SUGAR:** 3g

Feta, Tomato, and Broccolini

You may have noticed Broccolini showing up more and more in grocery stores as a tasty staple. It's been gaining popularity—for good reason! It is a little sweeter than its larger variety, with smaller stems and leaves, and provides a note of asparagus flavor.

Hands-On Time: 10 minutes
Cook Time: 6 minutes
Preheat Temperature: 350°F
Preheat Time: 3 minutes
Accessories/Prep: Fryer basket lined with parchment paper

Serves 2

1 bunch Broccolini, 1" trimmed from stalks
1 cup halved cherry tomatoes
1 tablespoon olive oil
¼ teaspoon salt
¼ cup crumbled feta cheese

1 In a large bowl, toss Broccolini and tomatoes with oil and salt.

2 Place Broccolini mixture in prepared fryer basket. Cook 6 minutes.

3 Transfer cooked Broccolini and tomatoes to a large serving dish. Garnish with feta. Serve warm.

PER SERVING

CALORIES: 145 | FAT: 11g | PROTEIN: 5g | SODIUM: 488mg | FIBER: 3g | CARBOHYDRATES: 8g | SUGAR: 4g

Togarashi Shishito Peppers

Although these sweet and smoky peppers are traditionally mild, one in ten peppers will be spicy, so tread lightly or make a game out of it! They can be eaten raw, but air frying gives them a little char that makes them taste even better. Add some sesame oil and a little togarashi, and you have hit each of the four taste zones, not to mention that elusive fifth: umami!

Hands-On Time: 5 minutes
Cook Time: 8 minutes
Preheat Temperature: 380°F
Preheat Time: 3 minutes
Accessories/Prep: Fryer basket

Serves 2

6 ounces shishito peppers
2 teaspoons sesame oil
1 teaspoon togarashi, divided

WHAT IS TOGARASHI?

Togarashi is a Japanese seven-spice blend that is becoming increasingly popular. If your local grocer doesn't carry it, specialty stores, Asian markets, and online stores are your place! Togarashi is well rounded with notes of pepper, bittersweet, brine, and citrus.

1 In a medium bowl, toss peppers with oil and ½ teaspoon togarashi.

2 Place peppers in fryer basket and cook 4 minutes. Shake basket, then cook 4 additional minutes or until peppers are blistered.

3 Transfer peppers to a large serving dish and garnish with remaining togarashi. Serve warm.

PER SERVING

CALORIES: 49 | FAT: 4g | PROTEIN: 2g | SODIUM: 0mg |
FIBER: 3g | CARBOHYDRATES: 6g | SUGAR: 3g

German Potato Salad

The tangy flavor of the vinegar is what sets a German potato salad apart from a traditional American mayonnaise-based recipe. Plus, unlike the American version, German potato salad is best served warm! Switch things up by serving this dish at your next picnic.

Hands-On Time: 15 minutes
Cook Time: 20 minutes
Preheat Temperature: 400°F
Preheat Time: 3 minutes
Accessories/Prep: Fryer basket

Serves 4

1 pound red potatoes, diced into 1" cubes
½ large yellow onion, peeled and diced
1 tablespoon olive oil
4 bacon strips, cooked and crumbled
2 tablespoons apple cider vinegar
2 teaspoons Dijon mustard
2 medium cloves garlic, peeled and minced
1 teaspoon granulated sugar
1 teaspoon salt
½ teaspoon ground black pepper
¼ cup chopped fresh parsley

1 In a large bowl, toss potatoes and onion in oil. Place in fryer basket and cook 10 minutes. Toss. Cook an additional 10 minutes.

2 Return potatoes to large bowl and toss with bacon, vinegar, mustard, garlic, sugar, salt, and pepper.

3 Garnish with parsley and serve warm.

PER SERVING

CALORIES: 166 | FAT: 7g | PROTEIN: 6g | SODIUM: 827mg | FIBER: 2g | CARBOHYDRATES: 20g | SUGAR: 3g

Jalapeño-Cheddar Pull-Apart Biscuits

Serve these jalapeño and cheese biscuit bites alongside your favorite eggs, a bowl of grits, and a thick slice of tomato for a well-rounded, hearty, and satisfying breakfast. Be warned that your family will scream for these savory, fluffy biscuits every weekend. A bonus: Leftovers are completely portable for busy mornings!

Hands-On Time: 10 minutes
Cook Time: 12 minutes
Preheat Temperature: 325°F
Preheat Time: 3 minutes
Accessories/Prep: Fryer basket; pizza pan sprayed with cooking spray

Serves 3

- ⅓ cup all-purpose flour
- ¼ teaspoon salt
- ¼ teaspoon baking powder
- 2 ounces cream cheese, room temperature
- ¼ cup shredded sharp Cheddar cheese
- 2 tablespoons drained jarred diced jalapeño peppers
- 1 teaspoon Dijon mustard
- 2 tablespoons whole buttermilk
- ½ teaspoon olive oil

1 In a medium bowl, combine flour, salt, and baking powder. In a small bowl, combine remaining ingredients. Add ingredients from small bowl to the dry ingredients in medium bowl. Do not overmix.

2 Form mixture into nine 1" balls and add to prepared pizza pan. Biscuits should touch. Place pan in fryer basket. Cook 12 minutes.

3 Transfer pan to a cooling rack. Serve warm.

PER SERVING

CALORIES: 168 | FAT: 10g | PROTEIN: 5g | SODIUM: 473mg | FIBER: 0g | CARBOHYDRATES: 12g | SUGAR: 1g

Haricots Verts

Literally translated to "green beans" in French, this variety is longer and slimmer than the traditional American green bean.

Hands-On Time: 5 minutes
Cook Time: 8 minutes
Preheat Temperature: 350°F
Preheat Time: 3 minutes
Accessories/Prep: Fryer basket

Serves 4

- 1/2 pound haricots verts, ends trimmed
- 2 teaspoons olive oil
- 1/2 teaspoon salt
- 1/4 teaspoon ground black pepper

1 In a medium bowl, toss haricots verts with oil, salt, and pepper.

2 Place haricots in fryer basket and cook 4 minutes. Shake fryer basket, then cook an additional 4 minutes.

3 Remove from basket and serve warm.

PER SERVING

CALORIES: 37 | FAT: 2g | PROTEIN: 1g | SODIUM: 293mg | FIBER: 2g | CARBOHYDRATES: 4g | SUGAR: 2g

Hasselback Baby Golds

If a baked potato and home fries had a baby, it would be the flavor combination you get in this dish. The butter cooks down in the potato, creating both a crisp and tender bite.

Hands-On Time: 15 minutes
Cook Time: 20 minutes
Preheat Temperature: 350°F
Preheat Time: 3 minutes
Accessories/Prep: Fryer basket

Serves 4

- 8 baby Yukon Gold potatoes
- 1 tablespoon olive oil
- 2 tablespoons unsalted butter, melted
- 1/4 teaspoon salt, divided
- 1/4 cup chopped fresh parsley

1 Make slices in the width of each potato about 1/4" apart without cutting all the way through potato. Brush sliced potatoes with oil, both outside and in between slices. Place potatoes in fryer basket. Cook 10 minutes.

2 Brush with melted butter, ensuring butter gets between slices. Season with 1/8 teaspoon salt. Cook an additional 10 minutes.

3 Transfer potatoes to a large serving dish. Season with remaining salt. Garnish with parsley. Serve warm.

PER SERVING

CALORIES: 158 | FAT: 9g | PROTEIN: 2g | SODIUM: 154mg | FIBER: 2g | CARBOHYDRATES: 18g | SUGAR: 1g

Sweet Potato Fries

Fries are great, but Sweet Potato Fries are on a whole other level. Filled with flavor and nutrition, you don't even feel like you are cheating, especially since the air fryer requires very little oil. Enjoy these with your choice of dipping sauce.

Hands-On Time: 10 minutes
Cook Time: 43 minutes
Preheat Temperature: 400°F
Preheat Time: 3 minutes
Accessories/Prep: Fryer basket

Serves 2

2 medium sweet potatoes, peeled and cut into 1/4" fries
1 tablespoon olive oil
2 teaspoons cornstarch
1/4 teaspoon garlic powder
1/4 teaspoon chili powder
1/2 teaspoon ground ginger
1/4 teaspoon salt

MAPLE-MUSTARD DIPPING SAUCE

There are many things you can dip your Sweet Potato Fries in, but you may want to give this one a try! Combine: 1/2 cup mayonnaise, 1/4 cup Dijon mustard, 1 tablespoon maple syrup, 1/2 teaspoon white wine vinegar, and 1/8 teaspoon each salt and ground black pepper. Taste and add more salt if necessary. Refrigerate while cooking fries.

1 In a large bowl, add fries and enough water to cover. Soak 30 minutes. Drain and dry completely.

2 In a medium bowl, toss fries with oil. Once coated, toss with cornstarch, garlic powder, chili powder, and ginger. Place fries in fryer basket and cook 8 minutes. Shake basket. Cook an additional 5 minutes.

3 Transfer fries to a bowl and season with salt. Serve warm.

PER SERVING

CALORIES: 175 | FAT: 7g | PROTEIN: 2g | SODIUM: 341mg | FIBER: 4g | CARBOHYDRATES: 27g | SUGAR: 7g

Shoestring French Fries

For best results, don't skip the soaking step. It helps eliminate some of the starch. This not only keeps the fries from sticking together, but also yields maximum crispiness!

Hands-On Time: 10 minutes
Cook Time: 42 minutes
Preheat Temperature: 400°F
Preheat Time: 3 minutes
Accessories/Prep: Fryer basket

Serves 4

2 medium russet potatoes (about 1 pound), cut into thin shoestring fries
2 teaspoons olive oil
3 teaspoons salt, divided
1 teaspoon smoked paprika

1 In a large bowl, add fries and enough water to cover. Soak 30 minutes. Drain and dry completely.

2 In a medium bowl, toss fries with oil and 1 teaspoon salt. Place fries in fryer basket and cook 6 minutes. Shake fryer basket, then cook an additional 6 minutes.

3 Transfer fries to a clean bowl and season with remaining salt and paprika. Serve warm.

PER SERVING

CALORIES: 105 | FAT: 2g | PROTEIN: 2g | SODIUM: 1,756mg | FIBER: 2g | CARBOHYDRATES: 19g | SUGAR: 1g

Garlic and Ginger Baby Bok Choy

Serve this dish next to a fillet of fresh fish to round out a healthy yet satisfying meal.

Hands-On Time: 10 minutes
Cook Time: 12 minutes
Preheat Temperature: 350°F
Preheat Time: 3 minutes
Accessories/Prep: Fryer basket

Serves 4

4 medium heads baby bok choy, trimmed and quartered lengthwise
1 tablespoon sesame oil
1/4 teaspoon minced fresh ginger
2 medium cloves garlic, peeled and minced
1/4 teaspoon salt

1 Brush bok choy with oil.

2 Place half of bok choy flat side down in fryer basket. Cook 5 minutes. Flip and sprinkle tops with ginger and garlic. Cook 1 additional minute, then transfer to a plate. Repeat with other half.

3 Season with salt and serve warm.

PER SERVING

CALORIES: 86 | FAT: 4g | PROTEIN: 6g | SODIUM: 418mg | FIBER: 4g | CARBOHYDRATES: 10g | SUGAR: 5g

Breaded Parmesan Zucchini Fries

These breaded, crispy zucchini fries will have you buying bags of zucchini just so you can keep making them. A healthy alternative to drive-through French fries, this treat satisfies that craving for deep-fried potatoes!

Hands-On Time: 10 minutes
Cook Time: 20 minutes
Preheat Temperature: 375°F
Preheat Time: 3 minutes
Accessories/Prep: Fryer basket lined with parchment paper

Serves 2

- 1 large zucchini, cut into ¼" fries
- ½ teaspoon salt
- 2 large eggs, whisked
- ½ cup panko bread crumbs
- ¼ cup grated Parmesan cheese
- 2 tablespoons cornstarch
- ½ teaspoon garlic powder

WHAT DIPPING SAUCE SHOULD I USE?

Although marinara is a favorite go-to dipping sauce for these delicious zucchini fries, you may want to experiment and try a Horseradish-Lemon Aioli. Combine the following: ½ cup mayonnaise, 4 teaspoons prepared horseradish, 2 teaspoons lemon zest, ¼ teaspoon lemon juice. Refrigerate until ready to use.

1 Scatter zucchini evenly over a paper towel. Sprinkle with salt. Let sit 10 minutes to pull out the moisture. Pat with paper towels.

2 Place whisked eggs in a shallow bowl. In a second shallow bowl, combine bread crumbs, Parmesan, cornstarch, and garlic powder. Dip a zucchini piece in whisked eggs. Shake off excess and dredge in bread crumb mixture. Shake off excess bread crumbs. Transfer to a plate and repeat with remaining zucchini.

3 Place half of zucchini in prepared fryer basket and cook 5 minutes. Gently flip fries. Cook an additional 5 minutes. Transfer to a serving dish. Repeat with remaining zucchini fries and serve warm.

PER SERVING

CALORIES: 195 | FAT: 6g | PROTEIN: 10g | SODIUM: 555mg | FIBER: 2g | CARBOHYDRATES: 26g | SUGAR: 5g

Roasted Potatoes

Whether you are adding these potatoes as a side to a steak, a piece of chicken, or a fresh salad, you really can't go wrong. These are superior to any potatoes you could make in your oven and make for a tasty side dish!

Hands-On Time: 5 minutes
Cook Time: 20 minutes
Preheat Temperature: 350°F
Preheat Time: 3 minutes
Accessories/Prep: Fryer basket

Serves 6

1 pound baby Yukon Gold
    potatoes, quartered
3 tablespoons unsalted
    butter, melted
$1/4$ teaspoon salt
$1/4$ teaspoon ground black
    pepper

1 In a large bowl, combine potatoes, butter, salt, and pepper.

2 Place potatoes in fryer basket. Cook 10 minutes. Toss potatoes. Cook an additional 10 minutes.

3 Transfer to a serving bowl and serve warm.

PER SERVING

CALORIES: 121 | FAT: 5g | PROTEIN: 2g | SODIUM: 105mg | FIBER: 2g | CARBOHYDRATES: 16g | SUGAR: 1g

Roasted Asparagus

Asparagus comes in varying versions of thickness. It can also be purchased white instead of green. No matter the size or color, the main thing to remember is to cut off the woody ends. After that, be sure to keep an eye on them as they cook, as the cooking time will vary.

Hands-On Time: 5 minutes
Cook Time: 8 minutes
Preheat Temperature: 400°F
Preheat Time: 3 minutes
Accessories/Prep: Fryer basket

Serves 4

16 thick spears asparagus,
    ends trimmed
2 teaspoons olive oil
$1/4$ teaspoon salt

1 In a large bowl, toss asparagus spears with oil. Season with salt.

2 Place spears in fryer basket. Cook 6–8 minutes or until cooked through.

3 Transfer to plates and serve warm.

PER SERVING

CALORIES: 32 | FAT: 2g | PROTEIN: 1g | SODIUM: 146mg | FIBER: 1g | CARBOHYDRATES: 2g | SUGAR: 1g

Mashed Potatoes with Thyme

The skins of the potatoes not only add nutrition to your mashed potatoes, but they also contribute to the texture and rustic flavor of the dish. The thyme, butter, and cream add pure luxury to these simple tubers.

Hands-On Time: 10 minutes
Cook Time: 14 minutes
Preheat Temperature: 350°F
Preheat Time: 3 minutes
Accessories/Prep: Fryer basket

Serves 4

1 pound Yukon Gold potatoes, diced into 1" cubes
3 tablespoons unsalted butter, divided
1/2 teaspoon salt
1/2 teaspoon ground black pepper
1/4 cup heavy cream
2 tablespoons fresh thyme leaves

HEAVY CREAM SUBSTITUTES

For a variety of reasons, such as diets or allergies, heavy cream is not always a desirable ingredient. Feel free to use any "milk" that fits your restrictions. Examples include whole milk, goat's milk, almond milk, and cashew milk.

1 In a large bowl, toss potatoes and 2 tablespoons butter.

2 Place potatoes in fryer basket. Cook 7 minutes. Shake basket. Cook an additional 7 minutes. Transfer to a large dish.

3 Mash the potatoes, salt, pepper, half the cream, thyme, and remaining butter. Slowly add remaining cream until potatoes reach desired consistency. Serve warm.

PER SERVING

CALORIES: 216 | FAT: 13g | PROTEIN: 3g | SODIUM: 303mg | FIBER: 3g | CARBOHYDRATES: 21g | SUGAR: 1g

Zucchini and Carrot Croquettes

Do you have any family members that tend to skew anti-vegetable? With these, you'll please both the vegetable haters and lovers! Chances are they'll never even know these crispy bites are baked with zucchini and carrots. To take these croquettes to the next level, serve them with sour cream as a simple dipping sauce.

Hands-On Time: 10 minutes
Cook Time: 22 minutes
Preheat Temperature: 350°F
Preheat Time: 3 minutes
Accessories/Prep: Fryer basket lined with parchment paper

Serves 6

- 1 1/2 cups grated zucchini
- 1/2 cup grated carrots
- 1/2 cup shredded Cheddar cheese
- 2 tablespoons minced yellow onion
- 1 tablespoon all-purpose flour
- 1 tablespoon cornmeal
- 1 tablespoon unsalted butter, melted
- 1 large egg, whisked
- 1/4 teaspoon salt
- 1/2 teaspoon ground black pepper
- 1 cup panko bread crumbs

1 Squeeze grated zucchini between paper towels to remove excess moisture and transfer to a large bowl. Add carrots, Cheddar, onion, flour, cornmeal, butter, egg, salt, and pepper. Stir to combine. Add bread crumbs to a separate shallow dish.

2 Form zucchini mixture into twelve balls, approximately 2 tablespoons each. Roll each ball in bread crumbs, covering all sides.

3 Place half of croquettes in prepared fryer basket. Cook 6 minutes. Flip croquettes and cook an additional 5 minutes. Transfer to a plate. Repeat with remaining croquettes. Serve warm.

PER SERVING

CALORIES: 136 | FAT: 6g | PROTEIN: 6g | SODIUM: 205mg | FIBER: 1g | CARBOHYDRATES: 14g | SUGAR: 2g

Blue Cheese and Chive Twice-Baked Potatoes

This is a side worthy of a special occasion. A decadent twice-baked potato, complete with creamy blue cheese, pairs perfectly with a juicy steak. But don't worry—if you want this with your regular weeknight meal, it works just as well!

Hands-On Time: 10 minutes
Cook Time: 47 minutes
Preheat Temperature: 400°F
Preheat Time: 3 minutes
Accessories/Prep: Fryer basket

Serves 4

2 teaspoons olive oil
2 medium russet potatoes (about 1 pound)
$1/2$ teaspoon salt
$1/4$ teaspoon ground black pepper
1 tablespoon unsalted butter
$1/2$ cup crumbled blue cheese
$1/4$ cup sour cream
1 tablespoon whole milk
$1/4$ cup chopped fresh chives

1 Rub oil over potatoes. Place in fryer basket. Cook 30 minutes. Flip potatoes. Cook an additional 15 minutes. Allow to sit until cool enough to handle.

2 Once cooled, slice each potato lengthwise. Scoop out potato into a large bowl, leaving $1/4$" layer of potato in skins. Keep skins intact. To the bowl with scooped potato, add salt, pepper, butter, blue cheese, sour cream, and milk. Mash ingredients together and spoon back into skins. Place in fryer basket and cook an additional 2 minutes.

3 Transfer potatoes to a plate. Garnish with chives and serve warm.

PER POTATO BOAT

CALORIES: 219 | FAT: 12g | PROTEIN: 6g | SODIUM: 504mg | FIBER: 2g | CARBOHYDRATES: 20g | SUGAR: 2g

Nectarine, Burrata, and Prosciutto Salad

This recipe is a five-star winner. Simple recipes tend to be the best, especially with fresh ingredients that can stand on their own. Here, air frying the nectarines brings out a sweetness that goes beautifully with the salty prosciutto and the creaminess of the Burrata.

Hands-On Time: 10 minutes
Cook Time: 5 minutes
Preheat Temperature: 350°F
Preheat Time: 3 minutes
Accessories/Prep: Fryer basket lined with parchment paper

Serves 2

2 medium nectarines, quartered and pitted
2 (4-ounce) balls fresh Burrata cheese
4 ounces prosciutto
2 teaspoons olive oil
2 teaspoons balsamic vinegar
4 fresh basil leaves, sliced
$\frac{1}{8}$ teaspoon salt
$\frac{1}{8}$ teaspoon ground black pepper

WHAT IS BURRATA?
Burrata is a mix of mozzarella and cream. The outer layer of mozzarella encloses a silky center of cream and fresh-stretched curds. Commercial varieties are often made from cow's milk, but it is an extra-special treat if you can find a ball made from the traditional water buffalo's milk.

1 Place nectarines in prepared fryer basket. Cook 5 minutes.

2 Transfer nectarines to two plates. Top with Burrata and prosciutto. Drizzle with oil and vinegar.

3 Garnish with basil, salt, and pepper. Serve immediately.

PER SERVING

CALORIES: 636 | FAT: 46g | PROTEIN: 34g | SODIUM: 716mg | FIBER: 2g | CARBOHYDRATES: 17g | SUGAR: 12g

Garlic Butter Prosciutto–Wrapped Asparagus

Enjoy this as a snack, side, or appetizer! When it comes to this combination, you can't go wrong. In this dish, the saltiness of the prosciutto lends just enough flavor for these tasty spears so that you don't need to add additional seasoning. It's a match made in heaven.

Hands-On Time: 10 minutes
Cook Time: 12 minutes
Preheat Temperature: 400°F
Preheat Time: 3 minutes
Accessories/Prep: Fryer basket sprayed with cooking spray

Serves 4

4 ounces prosciutto
16 thick spears asparagus, ends trimmed
2 tablespoons unsalted butter, melted
2 medium cloves garlic, peeled and minced

1 Slice prosciutto lengthwise into sixteen even slices. Wrap the prosciutto strips in a spiral from the bottom of each asparagus spear to the top, stopping before covering the tip.

2 Place wrapped asparagus in prepared fryer basket. In a small bowl, combine butter with garlic. Brush spears with garlic butter.

3 Cook 6 minutes. Gently shake basket. Cook an additional 6 minutes until prosciutto is crisp. Serve warm.

PER SERVING

CALORIES: 148 | FAT: 12g | PROTEIN: 8g | SODIUM: 115mg | FIBER: 1g | CARBOHYDRATES: 4g | SUGAR: 1g

Blistered Tomatoes

Heat brings out the natural sugars in tomatoes. Add these to your breakfast plate, atop pasta, alongside a grilled steak, or even with some air fryer chicken nuggets!

Hands-On Time: 5 minutes
Cook Time: 14 minutes
Preheat Temperature: 350°F
Preheat Time: 3 minutes
Accessories/Prep: Fryer basket

Serves 4

8 ounces (about 30) cherry tomatoes
2 teaspoons olive oil
¼ teaspoon salt
¼ teaspoon ground black pepper

1 In a small bowl, toss all ingredients.

2 Transfer tomatoes to fryer basket and cook 7 minutes. Shake basket. Cook an additional 7 minutes.

3 Transfer to a bowl and serve warm.

PER SERVING

CALORIES: 30 | FAT: 2g | PROTEIN: 1g | SODIUM: 148mg | FIBER: 1g | CARBOHYDRATES: 2g | SUGAR: 1g

Quartered Brussels Sprouts

If you tend to push Brussels sprouts aside due to the somewhat bitter flavor they're known for, try cooking them this way.

Hands-On Time: 10 minutes
Cook Time: 40 minutes
Preheat Temperature: 350°F
Preheat Time: 3 minutes
Accessories/Prep: Fryer basket sprayed with cooking spray

Serves 4

¼ cup freshly squeezed orange juice
1 tablespoon maple syrup
1 tablespoon olive oil
½ teaspoon salt
1 pound Brussels sprouts, trimmed and quartered

1 In a large bowl, whisk together orange juice, maple syrup, oil, and salt. Add Brussels sprouts and toss to coat. Refrigerate 30 minutes.

2 Place Brussels sprouts in prepared fryer basket. Cook 5 minutes. Toss, then cook an additional 5 minutes.

3 Transfer Brussels sprouts to a serving dish. Serve warm.

PER SERVING

CALORIES: 93 | FAT: 4g | PROTEIN: 4g | SODIUM: 316mg | FIBER: 4g | CARBOHYDRATES: 14g | SUGAR: 7g

5

Chicken Main Dishes

For many Americans, chicken comes in the form of nuggets, a bucket of greasy fried take-out, or the rotisserie variety that's already been cooked at the grocery store. You can certainly turn to these from time to time, but they're far from your only option—especially when you're armed with an air fryer. By making the switch, you'll make an impact on several areas of your life.

Let your air fryer become part of your weekly prep, not only saving money, but significantly reducing the amount of oil that is used (and that you're eating). Plus, the heat from the fryer lends crispiness on all sides, even sans oil. As an added bonus, because of the quicker cooking times, more nutrients stay intact and the chicken will be juicy and delicious.

From Grilled Chicken Bites and the Ultimate Chicken Salad to Chicken Parm Meatball Subs and Southern Fried Chicken Legs, this chapter has a little bit for everyone with simple air fryer recipes that can up your chicken game!

Grilled Chicken Bites

These chicken bites are great in salads, alongside your vegetables, or even as meal prep for the upcoming week of lunches and dinners. They go with just about anything. Although they're simple, they're quite tasty and are certain to become a staple in your kitchen.

Hands-On Time: 5 minutes
Cook Time: 9 minutes
Preheat Temperature: 350°F
Preheat Time: 3 minutes
Accessories/Prep: Fryer basket sprayed with cooking spray

Serves 4

2 (4-ounce) boneless, skinless chicken breasts, diced into 1" cubes
2 teaspoons olive oil
$1/2$ teaspoon salt
$1/4$ teaspoon ground black pepper

1 In a large bowl, toss chicken in oil. Season with salt and pepper.

2 Place chicken in prepared fryer basket and cook 4 minutes. Shake basket gently and flip chicken. Cook an additional 5 minutes. Check chicken using a meat thermometer to ensure internal temperature is at least 165°F.

3 Transfer chicken to a serving plate and let rest 5 minutes. Serve warm.

PER SERVING

CALORIES: 82 | FAT: 3g | PROTEIN: 13g | SODIUM: 311mg | FIBER: 0g | CARBOHYDRATES: 0g | SUGAR: 0g

Ultimate Chicken Salad

This combination of flavors is what gives this recipe the "ultimate" badge of honor and elevates it above a plain old chicken salad. Complete with lime juice, pecans, scallions, and raisins, this is a recipe you'll keep coming back to.

Hands-On Time: 10 minutes

Cook Time: 18 minutes

Preheat Temperature: 350°F

Preheat Time: 3 minutes

Accessories/Prep: Fryer basket sprayed with olive oil cooking spray

Serves 2

- 2 (8-ounce) boneless, skinless chicken breasts, diced into 1" cubes
- 1 teaspoon salt
- 1/4 teaspoon ground black pepper
- 1/2 cup mayonnaise
- 2 teaspoons Dijon mustard
- 1 teaspoon lime juice
- 1/4 cup chopped golden raisins
- 1 medium scallion, trimmed and sliced (green and white parts included)
- 2 tablespoons chopped pecans

1 Season chicken with salt and pepper. Place half of chicken in prepared fryer basket. Cook 4 minutes. Shake basket gently and flip chicken. Cook an additional 5 minutes. Use a meat thermometer to ensure internal temperature is at least 165°F.

2 Transfer chicken to a plate. Repeat with remaining chicken. Let rest 7 minutes until cool enough to handle.

3 In a large bowl, combine remaining ingredients. Add chicken and toss to coat thoroughly. Refrigerate covered up to 3 days.

PER SERVING

CALORIES: 368 | FAT: 10g | PROTEIN: 52g | SODIUM: 1,375mg | FIBER: 2g | CARBOHYDRATES: 19g | SUGAR: 13g

Honey Mustard Chicken-Arugula Salad

This is a salad that's both easy to prepare and sure to impress. This can be a weekday go-to while working from home, or it can be the dish you serve with friends paired with a fun drink and warm weather. Either way, it's sure to satisfy.

Hands-On Time: 5 minutes
Cook Time: 9 minutes
Preheat Temperature: 350°F
Preheat Time: 3 minutes
Accessories/Prep: Fryer basket sprayed with cooking spray

Serves 2

2 (4-ounce) boneless, skinless chicken breasts, diced into 1" cubes
2 teaspoons olive oil
$1/2$ teaspoon salt
$1/4$ teaspoon ground black pepper
$1/4$ cup mayonnaise
2 tablespoons yellow mustard
$1/4$ teaspoon apple cider vinegar
1 tablespoon honey
3 cups arugula
$1/4$ cup pecan pieces
$1/4$ cup blueberries

1 In a large bowl, toss chicken in oil. Season with salt and pepper.

2 Place chicken in prepared fryer basket and cook 4 minutes. Shake basket gently and flip chicken. Cook an additional 5 minutes. Check chicken using a meat thermometer to ensure internal temperature is at least 165°F.

3 In a separate large bowl, combine mayonnaise, mustard, vinegar, and honey. Toss with arugula and divide evenly between two bowls. Top salads with chicken, pecans, and blueberries. Serve immediately.

PER SERVING

CALORIES: 503 | FAT: 37g | PROTEIN: 28g | SODIUM: 977mg | FIBER: 3g | CARBOHYDRATES: 16g | SUGAR: 12g

Bang a Chicken Wontons

Sometimes tossed over fried shrimp, bang bang is a kind of preparation that is crispy, salty, creamy, tangy, and spicy. It is re-created here in a wonton with chicken. Whether served as a main dish, snack, or appetizer, this recipe is sure to please.

Hands-On Time: 30 minutes
Cook Time: 24 minutes
Preheat Temperature: 330°F
Preheat Time: 3 minutes
Accessories/Prep: Fryer basket

Serves 6

$^1/_3$ cup sweet chili sauce
1 tablespoon mayonnaise
1 teaspoon lime juice
$^1/_2$ teaspoon sriracha
$^1/_4$ teaspoon salt
3 medium cloves garlic, peeled and minced
1 cup shredded cooked chicken
$^1/_2$ cup bagged coleslaw mix (cabbage and carrots)
2 medium scallions, trimmed and finely chopped (white and green parts)
30 wonton wrappers
Olive oil cooking spray

1 In a medium bowl, whisk together sweet chili sauce, mayonnaise, lime juice, sriracha, and salt. Toss in garlic, chicken, and scallions (reserving some green parts for garnish) until combined.

2 Place 1 wonton wrapper on a cutting board. Place 2 teaspoons chicken mixture in the center of wrapper. Dip your finger in water and run it around the perimeter of the wonton. Fold one corner over to the opposite corner, forming a triangle. Press edges to seal. Repeat with remaining wontons and filling.

3 Place ten wontons in fryer basket and spray tops with cooking spray. Cook 8 minutes. Transfer to a plate. Repeat with remaining wontons. Serve warm with scallion greens as garnish.

PER SERVING

CALORIES: 212 | FAT: 3g | PROTEIN: 11g | SODIUM: 585mg | FIBER: 1g | CARBOHYDRATES: 33g | SUGAR: 8g

Kimchi Chicken Burgers

Ground chicken is known to make a dry burger; however, with the addition of kimchi, moisture and flavor are added to this otherwise bland meal. To top, mix a little gochujang sauce, according to your taste buds, with some mayonnaise and a splash of wine vinegar.

Hands-On Time: 10 minutes
Cook Time: 26 minutes
Preheat Temperature: 350°F
Preheat Time: 3 minutes
Accessories/Prep: Fryer basket sprayed with olive oil cooking spray

Serves 4

1 pound ground chicken
¼ cup kimchi
1 large egg white
¼ cup panko bread crumbs
1 teaspoon garlic powder
½ teaspoon granulated sugar
¼ teaspoon ground ginger
⅛ teaspoon salt

1 In a medium bowl, combine all ingredients and form four patties, making a slight indentation in the middle of each.

2 Place two patties in prepared fryer basket and cook 6 minutes. Flip and cook an additional 7 minutes. Check chicken using a meat thermometer to ensure internal temperature is at least 165°F. Transfer to a plate.

3 Repeat with remaining burgers. Serve warm.

PER BURGER

CALORIES: 204 | FAT: 9g | PROTEIN: 22g | SODIUM: 283mg | FIBER: 1g | CARBOHYDRATES: 9g | SUGAR: 2g

Easy Chicken Meatballs

Whether you eat them out of the fryer basket, toss them in sauce, or make a meatball hoagie, these chicken meatballs are versatile. You may want to steer clear of "white meat only" ground chicken. Stick with one that mixes dark and white meat to avoid dryness.

Hands-On Time: 15 minutes
Cook Time: 16 minutes
Preheat Temperature: 350°F
Preheat Time: 3 minutes
Accessories/Prep: Fryer basket sprayed with olive oil cooking spray

Serves 4

1 pound ground chicken
1 large egg
10 saltine crackers, crushed
¼ cup grated yellow onion
1 teaspoon Italian seasoning
½ teaspoon ground black
    pepper
¼ cup chopped fresh parsley

1 In a large bowl, combine chicken, egg, crackers, onion, Italian seasoning, and pepper. Form into eighteen meatballs, about 2 tablespoons each.

2 Place half of meatballs in prepared fryer basket and cook 4 minutes. Flip meatballs. Cook an additional 4 minutes. Check chicken using a meat thermometer to ensure internal temperature is at least 165°F. Transfer to a serving dish and repeat with remaining meatballs.

3 Garnish with chopped parsley. Serve warm.

PER SERVING

CALORIES: 215 | FAT: 10g | PROTEIN: 22g | SODIUM: 160mg | FIBER: 1g | CARBOHYDRATES: 7g | SUGAR: 1g

Chicken Cheesy Meatloaves

This is one of those recipes that is easy to fit into whatever dietary restrictions you adhere to. Using chicken instead of the traditional beef seen in meatloaf will satisfy the calorie counters. For the carb-conscious or gluten-free folks, change up the bread to a variety that meets your needs. You can even use dairy-free versions of the cheese and milk.

Hands-On Time: 15 minutes
Cook Time: 18 minutes
Preheat Temperature: 350°F
Preheat Time: 3 minutes
Accessories/Prep: Fryer basket sprayed with olive oil cooking spray; add 2 tablespoons water below basket

Serves 4

1 pound ground chicken
$1/4$ cup whole milk
1 cup diced day-old bread
$1/4$ cup whole-milk ricotta cheese
1 large egg
$1/4$ cup chopped fresh basil
1 teaspoon salt
$1/2$ teaspoon ground black pepper

FRESH BASIL SUBSTITUTE
Although there is no flavor substitute for the almighty basil leaf, in this recipe, feel free to use fresh parsley, spinach, or arugula. Each lends some freshness and nutrition to the loaves, just with different, but delicious, flavor notes.

1 In a large bowl, combine chicken with remaining ingredients. Form into two oval-shaped meatloaves.

2 Place loaves in prepared fryer basket and cook 18 minutes. Check chicken using a meat thermometer to ensure internal temperature is at least 165°F.

3 Transfer meatloaves to a cooling rack. Let cool 15 minutes. Slice and serve warm.

PER SERVING

CALORIES: 244 | FAT: 12g | PROTEIN: 25g | SODIUM: 737mg | FIBER: 0g | CARBOHYDRATES: 7g | SUGAR: 2g

Chicken Parm Meatball Subs

Who knew chicken Parm and meatball subs were a match made in heaven? The heartiness of the meatballs, the gooiness of the mozzarella, and the freshness of the marinara makes this sandwich a no-brainer. These subs are perfect for game day.

Hands-On Time: 15 minutes
Cook Time: 20 minutes
Preheat Temperature: 350°F
Preheat Time: 3 minutes
Accessories/Prep: Fryer basket sprayed with olive oil cooking spray

Serves 4

1 pound ground chicken
1 large egg
¼ cup Italian-style bread crumbs
¼ cup shredded Parmesan cheese
¼ cup grated yellow onion
¼ cup chopped fresh parsley
½ cup marinara sauce, plus ¼ cup for dipping
4 top-split hoagie rolls
4 (1-ounce) slices mozzarella cheese

1 In a large bowl, combine chicken, egg, bread crumbs, Parmesan, onion, and parsley. Form into sixteen meatballs. Place half of meatballs in prepared fryer basket and cook 4 minutes. Flip meatballs. Cook an additional 4 minutes. Check meatballs using a meat thermometer to ensure internal temperature is at least 165°F. Transfer to a plate, then repeat with remaining meatballs.

2 Divide ½ cup marinara evenly among hoagic rolls. Add four meatballs to each roll. Top with mozzarella slices and add two sandwiches to fryer basket. Cook 2 minutes or until cheese is melted. Transfer to plates, then repeat with remaining sandwiches.

3 Serve immediately with warmed marinara sauce for dipping.

PER SUB

CALORIES: 553 | FAT: 23g | PROTEIN: 40g | SODIUM: 919mg | FIBER: 4g | CARBOHYDRATES: 48g | SUGAR: 7g

Chicken–Green Chile Biscuit Balls

Although this recipe calls for canned white chicken, you can also use any leftover cooked meat you have, whether it's from a grocery store rotisserie chicken or even any prepped chicken you fixed earlier in the week. It's all about simple ingredients and big flavor.

Hands-On Time: 15 minutes
Cook Time: 15 minutes
Preheat Temperature: 320°F
Preheat Time: 3 minutes
Accessories/Prep: Fryer basket lined with aluminum foil

Serves 8

- 1 (16.3-ounce) can refrigerated oversized biscuits (8 total)
- 1 (10-ounce) can white chicken, drained
- 3 tablespoons cream cheese, room temperature
- 1 (4-ounce) can green chiles, drained
- 1/8 teaspoon salt
- 1/8 teaspoon ground black pepper

1 Open can of biscuits and separate on a cutting board. Roll out each biscuit into a circle about 1/4" thick.

2 In a medium bowl, combine chicken, cream cheese, chiles, salt, and pepper. In the center of each biscuit circle, spoon one-eighth of chicken mixture. Fold dough up to a point and pinch to seal. Place biscuits in prepared fryer basket seam side down.

3 Cook 15 minutes. Check chicken using a meat thermometer to ensure internal temperature is at least 165°F. Transfer to a cooling rack and let rest 5 minutes. Serve warm.

PER SERVING

CALORIES: 234 | FAT: 8g | PROTEIN: 9g | SODIUM: 829mg | FIBER: 2g | CARBOHYDRATES: 30g | SUGAR: 5g

Mushroom Chicken Pizzadillas

Pizza + Quesadilla = Pizzadilla! What else is there to say? With this fun combination you get the best of both worlds—all the flavors of pizza in an easy, portable tortilla. Make a stack for the group or let them add their own ingredients.

Hands-On Time: 15 minutes
Cook Time: 12 minutes
Preheat Temperature: 350°F
Preheat Time: 3 minutes
Accessories/Prep: Fryer basket; pizza pan sprayed with cooking spray

Serves 4

2 cups shredded cooked boneless, skinless chicken breast

$1/2$ teaspoon salt

1 teaspoon garlic powder

3 tablespoons unsalted butter, melted

8 (6") flour tortillas

1 cup marinara sauce

2 cups shredded mozzarella cheese

1 cup sliced white mushrooms

8 large fresh basil leaves, chopped

1 In a large bowl, toss chicken with salt and garlic powder.

2 Lightly brush melted butter on one side of 1 tortilla. Place tortilla butter side down in prepared pizza pan. Spread $1/4$ cup marinara sauce on tortilla. Layer $1/2$ cup chicken, $1/2$ cup mozzarella, $1/4$ cup mushrooms, and one-fourth of the basil leaves on sauce. Top with second tortilla. Lightly brush melted butter on top tortilla.

3 Place pizza pan in fryer basket and cook pizzadilla 3 minutes. Transfer pizzadilla to cooling rack and repeat with remaining tortillas and fillings. Slice each pizzadilla into six sections. Serve warm.

PER PIZZADILLA

CALORIES: 536 | FAT: 22g | PROTEIN: 38g | SODIUM: 1,339mg | FIBER: 3g | CARBOHYDRATES: 40g | SUGAR: 7g

Mustard Pretzel Chicken Nuggets

Take me out to the ball game! Who doesn't love a pretzel with that tangy yellow mustard? Add this to some nuggets and you can channel those ballpark flavors at home. The air fryer allows you to enjoy chicken nuggets without that deep-fried grease.

Hands-On Time: 15 minutes
Cook Time: 16 minutes
Preheat Temperature: 350°F
Preheat Time: 3 minutes
Accessories/Prep: Fryer basket sprayed with olive oil cooking spray

Serves 4

½ cup all-purpose flour
½ cup whole milk
2 tablespoons yellow mustard
1 cup crushed pretzels
2 boneless, skinless chicken breasts (about 1 pound), diced into 1" cubes

WHAT ARE "CRUSHED" PRETZELS?

When crushing pretzels, aim for the consistency of bread crumbs. This can be achieved by pulsing them in a food processor or blender. You can even put them in a sandwich bag and hit them with a rolling pin.

1 Place flour in a shallow dish. In a second shallow dish, whisk together milk and mustard. Add crushed pretzels to a third shallow dish.

2 Dredge chicken in flour. Dip in milk mixture, then roll in crushed pretzels. Place half of chicken nuggets in prepared fryer basket. Cook 4 minutes. Shake gently. Cook an additional 4 minutes. Check the chicken using a meat thermometer to ensure the internal temperature is at least 165°F. Transfer nuggets to a plate, then repeat with remaining chicken.

3 Serve warm.

PER SERVING

CALORIES: 260 | FAT: 4g | PROTEIN: 29g | SODIUM: 398mg | FIBER: 1g | CARBOHYDRATES: 26g | SUGAR: 2g

Balsamic Chicken Thighs

The balsamic vinegar used in the marinade for these chicken thighs adds a level of rich, complex sweetness. The olive oil and garlic temper that sweetness, and the basil grounds it all. And the chicken thighs? Well, their beautiful, fattier dark meat makes this recipe extra moist.

Hands-On Time: 5 minutes
Cook Time: 50 minutes
Preheat Temperature: 350°F
Preheat Time: 3 minutes
Accessories/Prep: Fryer basket sprayed with olive oil cooking spray

Serves 4

2 tablespoons olive oil
2 tablespoons balsamic vinegar
2 tablespoons honey
1 teaspoon dried basil
2 medium cloves garlic, peeled and minced
$1/2$ teaspoon salt
$1/4$ teaspoon ground black pepper
6 (3-ounce) boneless, skinless chicken thighs

CAN I FREEZE MARINATED CHICKEN THIGHS?

Absolutely! No matter what the marinade, add it to a gallon plastic bag with your chicken thighs. Press out any additional air before sealing and then lie flat in the freezer. Transfer the bag to your refrigerator the night before you'd like to prepare the dish and then cook per usual.

1 In a gallon-sized resealable plastic bag, combine oil, vinegar, honey, basil, garlic, salt, and pepper. Add chicken. Toss and massage in marinade. Refrigerate 30 minutes up to overnight.

2 Place chicken in prepared fryer basket and cook 10 minutes. Flip chicken and cook an additional 10 minutes. Check chicken using a meat thermometer to ensure internal temperature is at least 165°F. Transfer to a serving plate and let rest 5 minutes.

3 Transfer chicken to plates and serve warm.

PER SERVING

CALORIES: 325 | FAT: 16g | PROTEIN: 32g | SODIUM: 390mg | FIBER: 0g | CARBOHYDRATES: 11g | SUGAR: 10g

White Chicken Pizzas

White pizzas simply sub out the traditional pizza red sauce for a white sauce. To make this recipe easy, just pick up your favorite jarred Alfredo sauce. Adding chicken and fresh tomato, basil, and red onion makes you feel like you are at a pizza restaurant!

Hands-On Time: 10 minutes
Cook Time: 30 minutes
Preheat Temperature: 275°F
Preheat Time: 3 minutes
Accessories/Prep: Fryer basket; pizza pan sprayed with cooking spray

Serves 2

- ½ pound fresh pizza dough
- ½ cup Alfredo sauce
- 1 cup chopped cooked chicken
- ⅓ cup seeded and diced tomato
- 2 tablespoons chopped fresh basil
- 2 tablespoons finely diced red onion
- ½ cup shredded mozzarella cheese

1 Divide pizza dough in half. Press out one half of dough to fit prepared pizza pan, then place pan in fryer basket. Cook 5 minutes.

2 Remove pan and spread ¼ cup Alfredo sauce over dough up to ¼" from the edge. Evenly distribute ½ cup chicken, half of diced tomato, 1 tablespoon basil, and 1 tablespoon onion. Sprinkle ¼ cup mozzarella over pizza. Place in fryer basket and cook 10 minutes.

3 Gently transfer pizza to a cooling rack. Repeat with remaining dough and toppings. Slice pizzas and serve warm.

PER PIZZA

CALORIES: 584 | FAT: 21g | PROTEIN: 38g | SODIUM: 1,254mg | FIBER: 2g | CARBOHYDRATES: 60g | SUGAR: 9g

Potato Chip–Breaded Chicken Thighs

Although any potato chips could work with this recipe, the brininess of the dill pickle flavor takes these thighs to the next level. Simply grab a few handfuls, add them to a plastic bag, and crush them. You now have potato chip breading...voilà!

Hands-On Time: 5 minutes
Cook Time: 1 hour 22 minutes
Preheat Temperature: 380°F
Preheat Time: 3 minutes
Accessories/Prep: Fryer basket sprayed with olive oil cooking spray

Serves 4

½ cup whole buttermilk
4 (3-ounce) bone-in, skin-on chicken thighs
2 tablespoons cornstarch
2 tablespoons all-purpose flour
½ cup crushed dill pickle–flavored potato chips
Olive oil cooking spray

1 In a gallon-sized resealable plastic bag, combine buttermilk and chicken thighs. Seal bag and refrigerate 1 hour. Drain chicken thighs.

2 In a shallow bowl, combine cornstarch, flour, and potato chips. Dredge 1 chicken thigh in cornstarch mixture. Shake off excess mixture. Transfer to a plate and repeat with remaining chicken thighs. Place chicken in prepared fryer basket, spray tops of chicken with cooking spray, and cook 11 minutes. Flip chicken, spray again, and cook an additional 11 minutes. Check chicken using a meat thermometer to ensure internal temperature is at least 165°F.

3 Transfer thighs to a plate and serve warm.

PER SERVING

CALORIES: 225 | FAT: 9g | PROTEIN: 22g | SODIUM: 120mg | FIBER: 1g | CARBOHYDRATES: 11g | SUGAR: 1g

Boneless Chicken Thighs with Green Olives

This dish is reminiscent of a braised chicken dish that takes a lot of love and time. Skip the time, but keep the love. Serve up this healthy yet hearty meal alongside some mashed potatoes or the Roasted Potatoes recipe found in Chapter 4.

Hands-On Time: 10 minutes
Cook Time: 20 minutes
Preheat Temperature: 350°F
Preheat Time: 3 minutes
Accessories/Prep: Fryer basket and cake barrel

Serves 4

- 1 (15-ounce) can tomato sauce
- 1/2 teaspoon garlic powder
- 1 teaspoon smoked paprika
- 1 tablespoon manzanilla olive juice, from jar
- 1/2 medium yellow onion, peeled and sliced into half-moons
- 1/3 cup drained manzanilla olives
- 1 pound boneless, skinless chicken thighs
- 1 tablespoon olive oil
- 1/2 teaspoon salt
- 1/4 teaspoon ground black pepper

1 In a medium bowl, combine tomato sauce, garlic powder, paprika, and olive juice. Place in cake barrel. Scatter onion and olives over sauce. Add chicken thighs. Drizzle oil over chicken and season with salt and pepper.

2 Place cake barrel in fryer basket and cook 10 minutes. Flip chicken and cook an additional 10 minutes. Check chicken using a meat thermometer to ensure internal temperature is at least 165°F. Transfer to a serving plate and let rest 5 minutes.

3 Transfer chicken to plates and serve warm with olives and sauce.

PER SERVING

CALORIES: 385 | FAT: 18g | PROTEIN: 43g | SODIUM: 658mg | FIBER: 2g | CARBOHYDRATES: 8g | SUGAR: 4g

Barbecued Chicken Legs

This recipe allows you to choose your own sauce, whether homemade or store-bought. So if you have a specialty barbecue sauce recipe you swear by, this is the perfect excuse to use it. And if you don't, nobody has to know it's from the bottle! They'll be too busy licking their fingers to care anyway.

Hands-On Time: 5 minutes
Cook Time: 20 minutes
Preheat Temperature: 380°F
Preheat Time: 3 minutes
Accessories/Prep: Fryer basket sprayed with olive oil cooking spray

Serves 6

¼ cup cornstarch
⅓ cup all-purpose flour
1 teaspoon salt
6 bone-in, skin-on chicken legs (about 1½ pounds)
Olive oil cooking spray
½ cup barbecue sauce

1   In a shallow dish, combine cornstarch, flour, and salt. Dredge 1 chicken leg in mixture. Shake off excess. Transfer to a plate and repeat with remaining chicken legs.

2   Place chicken in prepared fryer basket. Spray tops of chicken with cooking spray and cook 9 minutes. Flip chicken, spray again, and cook an additional 9 minutes. Check chicken using a meat thermometer to ensure internal temperature is at least 165°F.

3   Transfer legs to a large bowl and add barbecue sauce. Toss to coat. Place back in fryer basket and cook an additional 2 minutes. Transfer to a plate and serve warm.

PER SERVING

CALORIES: 550 | FAT: 20g | PROTEIN: 63g | SODIUM: 885mg | FIBER: 0g | CARBOHYDRATES: 20g | SUGAR: 8g

Marinated Chicken Legs

You can't go wrong with this simple yet flavorful recipe. Once you try it out, you'll understand why. It will become a staple in your weeknight meal plans. You can freeze the chicken in the marinade for an even faster prep; thaw in the refrigerator the night before preparing the dish.

Hands-On Time: 5 minutes

Cook Time: 1 hour 18 minutes

Preheat Temperature: 380°F

Preheat Time: 3 minutes

Accessories/Prep: Fryer basket sprayed with olive oil cooking spray

Serves 4

- ¼ cup olive oil
- ¼ cup apple cider vinegar
- ¼ cup soy sauce
- 1 tablespoon balsamic vinegar
- 2 tablespoons packed light brown sugar
- 2 teaspoons Worcestershire sauce
- 1 tablespoon sriracha
- 4 medium cloves garlic, peeled and minced
- 1 teaspoon salt
- 8 bone-in, skin-on chicken drumsticks (about 2 pounds)

1 In a gallon-sized resealable plastic bag, combine oil, apple cider vinegar, soy sauce, balsamic vinegar, brown sugar, Worcestershire sauce, sriracha, garlic, and salt. Add chicken legs and massage in marinade. Refrigerate 1 hour up to overnight.

2 Place chicken in prepared fryer basket. Cook 9 minutes. Flip chicken and cook an additional 9 minutes. Check chicken using a meat thermometer to ensure internal temperature is at least 165°F.

3 Transfer chicken to a plate and serve warm.

PER SERVING

CALORIES: 512 | FAT: 28g | PROTEIN: 49g | SODIUM: 1,062mg | FIBER: 0g | CARBOHYDRATES: 6g | SUGAR: 4g

Southern Fried Chicken Legs

Ain't nothin' like a chicken leg from the south—especially if it has a little buttermilk, hot sauce, and crispy skin. Even though this isn't deep-fried in a cast iron pan, it tastes just as good, and it's healthier!

Hands-On Time: 5 minutes
Cook Time: 1 hour 22 minutes
Preheat Temperature: 380°F
Preheat Time: 3 minutes
Accessories/Prep: Fryer basket sprayed with olive oil cooking spray

Serves 4

½ cup whole buttermilk
2 teaspoons hot sauce
6 bone-in, skin-on chicken
 legs (about 1½ pounds)
¼ cup cornstarch
¼ cup all-purpose flour
2 teaspoons smoked paprika
1 teaspoon garlic salt
Olive oil cooking spray

1 In a gallon-sized resealable plastic bag, combine buttermilk and hot sauce. Add chicken legs and toss to coat. Seal bag and refrigerate 1 hour. Drain chicken legs.

2 In a shallow dish, combine cornstarch, flour, paprika, and garlic salt. Dredge 1 chicken leg in mixture. Shake off excess. Transfer to a plate and repeat with remaining chicken legs.

3 Place chicken in prepared fryer basket, spray tops of chicken with cooking spray, and cook 11 minutes. Flip chicken, spray again, and cook an additional 11 minutes. Check chicken using a meat thermometer to ensure internal temperature is at least 165°F. Transfer legs to a plate and serve warm.

PER SERVING

CALORIES: 770 | FAT: 31g | PROTEIN: 94g | SODIUM: 802mg | FIBER: 1g | CARBOHYDRATES: 12g | SUGAR: 1g

Apricot-Dijon Chicken Tenders

Jams and jellies are a quick and easy way to impart some fruit and sweetness into savory meals. Add the air fryer for a healthy way to crisp up these tenders, and you have two kitchen hacks in one!

Hands-On Time: 10 minutes
Cook Time: 15 minutes
Preheat Temperature: 400°F
Preheat Time: 3 minutes
Accessories/Prep: Fryer basket lined with parchment paper

Serves 4

- ⅓ cup apricot jam
- 2 tablespoons Dijon mustard
- ¼ teaspoon salt
- ¼ teaspoon ground black pepper
- 1 pound chicken tenders

WHAT ARE CHICKEN TENDERS?
Chicken tenders are simply chicken breast sliced into long tenders. Most grocers sell them as tenders; however, if you can't find them, simply purchase some boneless, skinless breasts and cut them into long slices about 1" wide.

1. In a large bowl, whisk together jam, mustard, salt, and pepper. Set aside.

2. Place chicken in prepared fryer basket and cook 5 minutes. Flip chicken, then cook an additional 5 minutes. Flip chicken a final time and cook a final 5 minutes. Check chicken using a meat thermometer to ensure internal temperature is at least 165°F.

3. Transfer cooked chicken to whisked marinade and gently toss to coat. Serve warm.

PER SERVING

CALORIES: 174 | FAT: 1g | PROTEIN: 22g | SODIUM: 447mg | FIBER: 0g | CARBOHYDRATES: 18g | SUGAR: 12g

Traditional Buffalo Hot Wings

If you use your air fryer for only one food, make it chicken wings! The convection heat cooks the chicken skin on all sides, making each bite crispy on the outside and juicy on the inside. These wings may be even better than the ones from your favorite sports bar.

Hands-On Time: 10 minutes
Cook Time: 18 minutes
Preheat Temperature: 400°F
Preheat Time: 3 minutes
Accessories/Prep: Fryer basket; add 1 tablespoon water below basket

Serves 6

2 pounds chicken wings, split at the joints
1 tablespoon olive oil
1 tablespoon unsalted butter, room temperature
½ cup buffalo wing sauce

BLUE CHEESE DIPPING SAUCE
For a homemade blue cheese dipping sauce, combine 1 cup plain Greek yogurt; 1 tablespoon mayonnaise; ⅓ cup blue cheese crumbles; 2 peeled, minced garlic cloves; ½ teaspoon salt; 1 teaspoon lemon juice; ½ teaspoon Worcestershire sauce; and 2 teaspoons dried chopped chives. Refrigerate covered until ready to use. If you prefer a thinner sauce (or dressing for a salad), add 1 tablespoon milk at a time until desired consistency is reached.

1 Toss wings in olive oil and place in prepared fryer basket. Cook 9 minutes. Flip wings and cook an additional 9 minutes. Check chicken using a meat thermometer to ensure internal temperature is at least 165°F.

2 While wings are cooking, add butter and buffalo win sauce to a large bowl and mix until smooth.

3 Toss cooked wings in sauce and butter. Let cool 5 minutes. Serve warm.

PER SERVING

CALORIES: 148 | FAT: 11g | PROTEIN: 11g | SODIUM: 656mg | FIBER: 0g | CARBOHYDRATES: 0g | SUGAR: 0g

Sweet and Spicy Chicken Wings

This dish has a little bit of sweet from the honey and a little bit of spice from the hot mustard. The combination of all the flavors makes these wings come to life in your mouth. Want a little hack? Save some of those hot mustard packets from your Chinese takeout and use them in this recipe! You won't regret it.

Hands-On Time: 10 minutes
Cook Time: 18 minutes
Preheat Temperature: 400°F
Preheat Time: 3 minutes
Accessories/Prep: Fryer basket

Serves 4

1 tablespoon sesame oil
2 tablespoons spicy yellow mustard
1 tablespoon soy sauce
1 tablespoon honey
1 teaspoon rice vinegar
2 pounds chicken wings, split at the joints

1 In a large bowl, whisk together oil, mustard, soy sauce, honey, and vinegar. Toss wings in sauce to coat.

2 Place wings in fryer basket. Cook 9 minutes. Flip wings, then cook an additional 9 minutes. Check chicken using a meat thermometer to ensure internal temperature is at least 165°F.

3 Transfer to a plate and let cool 5 minutes. Serve warm.

PER SERVING

CALORIES: 220 | FAT: 14g | PROTEIN: 16g | SODIUM: 370mg | FIBER: 0g | CARBOHYDRATES: 5g | SUGAR: 4g

HOW TO SEPARATE CHICKEN WINGS

Some grocery stores will sell chicken wings already split; however, sometimes you may have to purchase whole wings. To separate, stretch the wing out. Using kitchen shears or a sharp knife, cut the portions at the joints to yield a drumette, wingette, and tip. The tips are not typically used in prepared chicken wings, so you can use them to make broth or season soups.

Mediterranean Chicken Wings

If you were dining alfresco on the island of Capri, drinking a glass of wine, and enjoying the view of the sea, these would be your wings. Simple, tasty, authentic.

Hands-On Time: 10 minutes
Cook Time: 18 minutes
Preheat Temperature: 400°F
Preheat Time: 3 minutes
Accessories/Prep: Fryer basket sprayed with olive oil cooking spray

Serves 4

1 tablespoon olive oil
1 tablespoon balsamic vinegar
2 tablespoons grated Parmesan cheese
1¹⁄₂ pounds chicken wings, split at the joints

1 In a large bowl, whisk together oil, vinegar, and Parmesan. Toss wings in sauce.

2 Place wings in prepared fryer basket. Cook 9 minutes. Flip wings, then cook an additional 9 minutes. Check chicken using a meat thermometer to ensure internal temperature is at least 165°F.

3 Transfer to a plate and let cool 5 minutes. Serve warm.

PER SERVING

CALORIES: 170 | FAT: 12g | PROTEIN: 13g | SODIUM: 94mg | FIBER: 0g | CARBOHYDRATES: 1g | SUGAR: 1g

6

Beef and Pork Main Dishes

Naturally gluten-free—which fits into many current diets—beef and pork are two meats that crisp up nicely in the air fryer and are both absolutely mouthwatering and delicious. They also contain protein and naturally healthy fats, two of the three macronutrients our bodies need to survive.

From Cowgirl Filet Mignons and Steak Taco Bowls to Peachy Pork Chops and Cubano Tortilla Wraps, this chapter is filled with a variety of easy-to-follow recipes that will cut down on your prep time but not on the flavors.

Santa Fe Eggrolls

This Mexican-Asian fusion is a must. These self-contained crunchy vessels deliver beef, beans, and corn with a taco seasoning and some gooey cheese right to your mouth! They're a crowd-pleaser your guests have probably never seen before.

Hands-On Time: 20 minutes
Cook Time: 29 minutes
Preheat Temperature: 350°F
Preheat Time: 3 minutes
Accessories/Prep: Fryer basket lined with parchment paper

Serves 12

2 teaspoons olive oil
½ pound ground beef
2 medium scallions, trimmed and sliced thin (green and white parts included)
1 (11-ounce) can corn, drained
1 (15-ounce) can black beans, drained and rinsed
2 medium Roma tomatoes, diced small
1 tablespoon taco seasoning
½ teaspoon salt
2 cups shredded Mexican-blend cheese
12 eggroll wrappers
Olive oil cooking spray

1 In a medium saucepan over medium heat, add oil, beef, and scallions. Cook 3–5 minutes until beef is no longer pink. Add corn, beans, tomatoes, taco seasoning, salt, and cheese. Remove from heat and let mixture cool completely.

2 Place 1 eggroll wrapper on a work surface. Place 2 tablespoons beef mixture in center of wrapper. Fold ½" of both ends of wrapper over mixture. Roll lengthwise to form an eggroll and transfer seam side down to a plate. Repeat with remaining beef mixture and wrappers.

3 Place six eggrolls seam side down in prepared fryer basket. Spray tops with cooking spray. Cook 9 minutes. Flip eggrolls and cook an additional 3 minutes. Transfer eggrolls seam side down to a cooling rack. Repeat with remaining eggrolls. Serve warm.

PER SERVING

CALORIES: 249 | FAT: 8g | PROTEIN: 14g | SODIUM: 519mg | FIBER: 4g | CARBOHYDRATES: 28g | SUGAR: 1g

Steak and Blue Cheese Grits

The rib eye, cut from the rib area of the animal, is beautifully marbled. Because of this extra fat, the taste is amazing. Be sure to add the tablespoon of water beneath the air fryer basket. When the fat renders down, the water will help keep the fat drippings from smoking.

Hands-On Time: 15 minutes
Cook Time: 10 minutes
Preheat Temperature: 400°F
Preheat Time: 3 minutes
Accessories/Prep: Fryer basket lined with parchment paper; add 1 tablespoon water below basket

Serves 2

- $1/2$ teaspoon salt
- $1/4$ teaspoon ground black pepper
- $1/4$ teaspoon garlic powder
- $1/4$ teaspoon smoked paprika
- 1 (1"-thick) rib eye steak (about 12 ounces)
- 3 cups cooked grits
- 2 tablespoons crumbled blue cheese
- 2 tablespoons chopped fresh parsley

1 In a small bowl, combine salt, pepper, garlic powder, and paprika. Season steak on both sides with mixture. Place steak in prepared fryer basket and cook 5 minutes. Flip steak and cook an additional 5 minutes. This should yield a medium-rare steak. Due to differences in steak sizes and doneness preferences, check steak with a meat thermometer to ensure satisfaction.

2 While steak is cooking, prepare grits according to package instructions. When complete, toss in blue cheese. Divide grits mixture evenly between two bowls.

3 Transfer steak to a cutting board and let rest 5 minutes. Slice thinly across the grain and transfer to the top of grits. Garnish with parsley and serve warm.

PER SERVING

CALORIES: 530 | FAT: 16g | PROTEIN: 43g | SODIUM: 763mg | FIBER: 3g | CARBOHYDRATES: 50g | SUGAR: 0g

Swirled Corn Dogs with Blueberry Ketchup

Of course you can dip these corn dogs in regular ketchup, buy why? This blueberry version is not only strong on nutrition, but the flavor offers a tasty variation.

Hands-On Time: 5 minutes
Cook Time: 40 minutes
Preheat Temperature: 380°F
Preheat Time: 3 minutes
Accessories/Prep: Fryer basket lined with parchment paper

Serves 6

1 cup blueberries
1 tablespoon lime juice
¼ large sweet onion, peeled
½ cup granulated sugar
2 tablespoons white wine vinegar
½ teaspoon ground ginger
⅛ teaspoon salt
1 (11-ounce) can refrigerated Cornbread Swirls rolls
6 beef hot dogs

1 In a food processor, pulse blueberries, lime juice, onion, sugar, vinegar, ginger, and salt. Refrigerate covered for 30 minutes or up to 2 weeks.

2 Open can of Cornbread Swirls and separate rolls. For each corn dog, unroll a dough piece and wrap dough around hot dog in a spiral.

3 Place corn dogs in prepared fryer basket and cook 10 minutes. Transfer to a cooling rack. Serve corn dogs warm with chilled blueberry ketchup.

PER CORN DOG

CALORIES: 407 | FAT: 19g | PROTEIN: 9g | SODIUM: 887mg | FIBER: 1g | CARBOHYDRATES: 45g | SUGAR: 25g

Cowgirl Filet Mignons

The cowboys can't have all the fun. All this cut of steak needs is a simple rub and some heat from your air fryer. The result is arguably better than anything you could do with your stove, and you'll be doing this beautiful cut of meat justice.

Hands-On Time: 15 minutes
Cook Time: 12 minutes
Preheat Temperature: 375°F
Preheat Time: 3 minutes
Accessories/Prep: Fryer basket lined with parchment paper; add 1 tablespoon water below basket

Serves 2

Cowgirl Marinade
¼ cup olive oil
½ teaspoon salt
½ teaspoon ground cumin
½ teaspoon chili powder
½ teaspoon garlic powder
½ teaspoon instant espresso powder

Steaks
2 (1½"-thick) filet mignon steaks (about 1 pound)
1 tablespoon unsalted butter, cut into 2 pats

1. In a small bowl, combine Cowgirl Marinade ingredients. Season steaks on both sides with marinade.

2. Place steaks in prepared fryer basket and cook 6 minutes. Flip steaks and cook an additional 6 minutes. This should yield medium-rare steaks. Due to differences in steak sizes and doneness preferences, check steak with a meat thermometer to ensure satisfaction.

3. Transfer steaks to a cutting board and top each with 1 pat of butter. Let rest 5 minutes before serving.

PER STEAK

CALORIES: 655 | FAT: 46g | PROTEIN: 56g | SODIUM: 709mg | FIBER: 1g | CARBOHYDRATES: 1g | SUGAR: 0g

Sage Garlic Butter Strip Steaks

The herbal flavor of sage holds up against the garlic and butter infusing these steaks. Serve them next to some Haricots Verts or Hasselback Baby Golds (or both!) from Chapter 4.

Hands-On Time: 5 minutes
Cook Time: 8 minutes
Preheat Temperature: 400°F
Preheat Time: 3 minutes
Accessories/Prep: Fryer basket lined with parchment paper; add 1 tablespoon water below basket

Serves 2

2 (8-ounce) strip steaks
1 teaspoon salt
½ teaspoon ground black pepper
3 tablespoons unsalted butter, melted
3 medium cloves garlic, peeled and minced
2 teaspoons ground sage

1 Season both sides of steaks with salt and pepper. Place steaks in prepared fryer basket and cook 4 minutes. Flip steaks and cook an additional 4 minutes. This should yield medium-rare steaks. Due to differences in steak sizes and doneness preferences, check steak with a meat thermometer to ensure satisfaction. Transfer to cutting board and let rest 5 minutes.

2 While steak is resting, in a small bowl, combine melted butter, garlic, and sage.

3 Slice steaks. Pour butter mixture over steaks and serve warm.

PER SERVING

CALORIES: 554 | FAT: 39g | PROTEIN: 36g | SODIUM: 12mg | FIBER: 1g | CARBOHYDRATES: 2g | SUGAR: 0g

Seasoned Flank Steak

Flank steak is such an underrated cut of beef. It's inexpensive, yet delicious. All this cut needs is a little marinade and then proper slicing. Once rested, cut the flank steak thinly across the grain.

Hands-On Time: 5 minutes
Cook Time: 19 minutes
Preheat Temperature: 325°F
Preheat Time: 3 minutes
Accessories/Prep: Fryer basket lined with parchment paper; add 1 tablespoon water below basket

Serves 4

¼ cup olive oil
½ teaspoon salt
¼ teaspoon ground black pepper
1 teaspoon smoked paprika
½ teaspoon ground cumin
½ teaspoon garlic powder
1 tablespoon packed light brown sugar
1 (1-pound) flank steak

1 In a gallon-sized resealable plastic bag, combine oil, salt, pepper, paprika, cumin, garlic powder, and brown sugar. Add flank steak and seal. Massage marinade into steak. Refrigerate 30 minutes up to overnight. Drain steak.

2 Place steak in prepared fryer basket and cook 10 minutes. Flip steak and cook an additional 9 minutes. This should yield a medium-rare steak. Due to differences in steak sizes and doneness preferences, check steak with a meat thermometer to ensure satisfaction.

3 Transfer steak to a cutting board. Let rest 5 minutes before serving. Slice thinly against the grain for maximum tenderness. Serve warm.

PER SERVING

CALORIES: 322 | FAT: 21g | PROTEIN: 26g | SODIUM: 340mg | FIBER: 0g | CARBOHYDRATES: 4g | SUGAR: 3g

Steak Taco Bowls

Brimming with flavor, these Steak Taco Bowls are where it's at. The coolness of the tomatoes, lettuce, and guacamole is refreshing against the spicy sriracha mayonnaise. If you find the mayonnaise to be too thick, add another teaspoon or two of water for drizzling consistency.

Hands-On Time: 5 minutes
Cook Time: 49 minutes
Preheat Temperature: 325°F
Preheat Time: 3 minutes
Accessories/Prep: Fryer basket; add 1 tablespoon water below basket

Serves 4

1/3 cup mayonnaise
1 tablespoon sriracha
1 teaspoon water
1/4 cup olive oil
1/2 teaspoon salt
2 tablespoons taco seasoning
1 (1-pound) flank steak
4 cups shredded iceberg lettuce
1 cup shredded Cheddar cheese
2 medium Roma tomatoes, diced
1/2 cup guacamole

1 In a small bowl, whisk together mayonnaise, sriracha, and water. Set aside in refrigerator. In a gallon-sized resealable plastic bag, combine oil, salt, and taco seasoning. Add steak, seal bag, and toss to coat. Refrigerate 30 minutes up to overnight. Drain steak.

2 Place steak in prepared fryer basket and cook 10 minutes. Flip steak and cook an additional 9 minutes. This should yield a medium-rare steak. Due to differences in steak sizes and doneness preferences, check steak with a meat thermometer to ensure satisfaction. Transfer meat to a cutting board and let rest 5 minutes. Thinly slice meat against the grain.

3 Divide lettuce evenly among four bowls. Evenly add Cheddar, tomatoes, and guacamole. Top bowls with sliced steak and drizzle with sriracha mayonnaise. Serve.

PER BOWL

CALORIES: 539 | FAT: 38g | PROTEIN: 34g | SODIUM: 935mg | FIBER: 2g | CARBOHYDRATES: 8g | SUGAR: 3g

Herbed Pork Loin Roast

Fall is in the air! The herbs in this recipe are reminiscent of holiday flavors, and a roast is always so comforting. Because the loin roast is a less fatty cut, it is necessary to check the internal temperature toward the end of cooking. If overcooked, the roast can become dry. If cooked correctly, it is heaven!

Hands-On Time: 10 minutes
Cook Time: 40 minutes
Preheat Temperature: 350°F
Preheat Time: 3 minutes
Accessories/Prep: Fryer basket lined with parchment paper; add 1 tablespoon water below basket

Serves 6

1 tablespoon olive oil
1 (2-pound) boneless pork loin roast
1 teaspoon dried rosemary
1 teaspoon dried basil
1 teaspoon dried thyme
$\frac{1}{2}$ teaspoon garlic powder
$\frac{1}{2}$ teaspoon salt
$\frac{1}{4}$ teaspoon ground black pepper

1 On a cutting board, massage oil over loin roast. In a small bowl, combine rosemary, basil, thyme, garlic powder, salt, and pepper. Season oiled roast with spices.

2 Place pork in prepared fryer basket and cook 20 minutes. Flip and cook an additional 20 minutes. Check pork using a meat thermometer to ensure internal temperature is at least 145°F.

3 Transfer pork to a cutting board and let rest 5 minutes. Slice and serve warm.

PER SERVING

CALORIES: 245 | FAT: 10g | PROTEIN: 35g | SODIUM: 270mg | FIBER: 0g | CARBOHYDRATES: 1g | SUGAR: 0g

Greek Steak Salad

For meat lovers, steak salads are a great way to enjoy one of your favorite foods while still getting plenty of nutrients. You don't have to be a strictly meat and potatoes person to appreciate this dish. It's not only hearty but also filled with flavors and salad additions that deliver on all notes.

Hands-On Time: 5 minutes
Cook Time: 49 minutes
Preheat Temperature: 325°F
Preheat Time: 3 minutes
Accessories/Prep: Fryer basket; add 1 tablespoon water below basket

Serves 4

- ¼ cup plus 1 tablespoon olive oil, divided
- ¼ cup plain Greek yogurt
- 1½ teaspoons salt, divided
- 1 teaspoon red pepper flakes
- 1 (1-pound) flank steak
- 4 cups chopped romaine lettuce
- ½ teaspoon ground black pepper
- 1 tablespoon red wine vinegar
- 4 tablespoons crumbled feta cheese
- ½ medium red onion, peeled and thinly sliced into half-moons
- ½ cup kalamata olives, pitted and chopped
- ½ medium English cucumber, trimmed and diced small

1 In a gallon-sized resealable plastic bag, combine ¼ cup oil, yogurt, 1 teaspoon salt, and red pepper flakes. Add steak, seal bag, and toss to coat. Refrigerate 30 minutes up to overnight. Drain steak; discard marinade.

2 Place steak in prepared fryer basket and cook 10 minutes. Flip steak and cook an additional 9 minutes. This should yield a medium-rare steak. Due to differences in steak sizes and doneness preferences, check steak with a meat thermometer to ensure satisfaction. Transfer steak to a cutting board and let rest 5 minutes. Slice thinly across the grain for maximum tenderness.

3 While steak is resting, add lettuce to a large bowl. Season with remaining salt and black pepper. Slowly drizzle in remaining oil and vinegar. Toss to mix well and divide evenly among four bowls. Evenly add feta, onion, olives, and cucumber. Top with sliced steak and serve warm.

PER SERVING

CALORIES: 361 | FAT: 24g | PROTEIN: 28g | SODIUM: 953mg | FIBER: 1g | CARBOHYDRATES: 5g | SUGAR: 2g

Barbecued Beef Short Ribs

These ribs will taste like they were cooked "low and slow," the way they're supposed to be, but the air fryer allows you to cut way down on the cook time! When people start asking for your secret to the perfect short ribs, you can point to your appliance.

Hands-On Time: 10 minutes
Cook Time: 46 minutes
Preheat Temperature: 380°F
Preheat Time: 3 minutes
Accessories/Prep: Fryer basket lined with parchment paper; add 1 tablespoon water below basket

Serves 2

1 cup barbecue sauce
1 pound beef short ribs

1. In a gallon-sized resealable plastic bag, combine barbecue sauce and ribs. Seal bag and toss to coat. Refrigerate 30 minutes up to overnight. Drain ribs; reserve marinade.

2. Place ribs in prepared fryer basket. Cook 8 minutes. Flip ribs and brush with reserved marinade. Cook an additional 8 minutes.

3. Transfer ribs to a plate and serve warm.

PER SERVING

CALORIES: 555 | FAT: 18g | PROTEIN: 38g | SODIUM: 1,565mg | FIBER: 1g | CARBOHYDRATES: 58g | SUGAR: 48g

Hawaiian Pizza

This recipe can start a fight on *Twitter* quicker than politics! So, this recipe is strictly for those people who love this tropical combination.

Hands-On Time: 10 minutes
Cook Time: 15 minutes
Preheat Temperature: 275°F
Preheat Time: 3 minutes
Accessories/Prep: Fryer basket and pizza pan

Serves 1

1/4 pound fresh pizza dough
2 tablespoons marinara sauce
1/4 cup cubed cooked ham
1/4 cup diced pineapple
1/4 cup shredded part-skim
   mozzarella cheese

1. Press out dough to fit pizza pan. Place pan in fryer basket and cook 5 minutes.

2. Remove pan and spread marinara over dough up to 1/4" from the edge. Add ham cubes and pineapple. Sprinkle mozzarella over pizza. Cook an additional 10 minutes.

3. Gently transfer pizza to a cutting board. Cut into slices and serve.

PER PIZZA

CALORIES: 455 | FAT: 10g | PROTEIN: 22g | SODIUM: 1,401mg | FIBER: 3g | CARBOHYDRATES: 68g | SUGAR: 18g

Cheeseburger Sliders

Sometimes a slider sounds much more inviting than an entire burger. Plus, they're just plain cute. Now that small slider buns have become available in most grocery stores, these teeny burgers are easier to add to your rotation.

Hands-On Time: 10 minutes
Cook Time: 18 minutes
Preheat Temperature: 350°F
Preheat Time: 3 minutes
Accessories/Prep: Fryer basket; fryer grill pan sprayed with cooking spray; add 1 tablespoon water below basket

Serves 4

1 pound ground beef
$1/3$ cup grated yellow onion
$1/2$ teaspoon smoked paprika
$1/2$ teaspoon salt
$1/4$ teaspoon ground black pepper
$1/3$ cup shredded Cheddar cheese
8 slider buns

1 In a medium bowl, combine beef, onion, paprika, salt, pepper, and Cheddar. Form into eight slider-sized patties. Make a slight indentation in the middle of each slider as the beef will rise during cooking.

2 Place four sliders on prepared grill pan and place into fryer basket. Cook 5 minutes. Flip sliders and cook an additional 4 minutes or until desired doneness, which can be checked with a meat thermometer. Transfer sliders to buns, then repeat with remaining sliders.

3 Serve warm.

PER SERVING

CALORIES: 445 | FAT: 17g | PROTEIN: 32g | SODIUM: 701mg | FIBER: 2g | CARBOHYDRATES: 37g | SUGAR: 6g

Blue Plate Special Mini Meatloaves

Splitting your meatloaf into two loaves not only takes less time to bake, but there are more crispy edges. Enjoy this traditional blue plate special with mashed potatoes and gravy or slice it up for a meatloaf sandwich!

Hands-On Time: 15 minutes
Cook Time: 18 minutes
Preheat Temperature: 350°F
Preheat Time: 3 minutes
Accessories/Prep: Fryer basket sprayed with olive oil cooking spray; add 1 tablespoon water below basket

Serves 4

Meatloaves
1 pound ground beef
1 tablespoon Dijon mustard
1 large whisked egg
1/3 cup panko bread crumbs
2 tablespoons whole milk
1 large carrot, peeled and finely grated
1/4 cup chopped fresh parsley
1/2 teaspoon salt
1/2 teaspoon ground black pepper

Topping
2 tablespoons ketchup
1/2 teaspoon yellow mustard
1/4 teaspoon Worcestershire sauce

1 To make Meatloaves, combine beef, mustard, egg, bread crumbs, milk, carrot, parsley, salt, and pepper in a large bowl. Form into two oval-shaped loaves.

2 In a small bowl, combine Topping ingredients and brush on top of loaves. Place in prepared fryer basket and cook 18 minutes.

3 Transfer Meatloaves to a cooling rack and let rest 15 minutes. Slice and serve warm.

PER SERVING

CALORIES: 284 | FAT: 12g | PROTEIN: 26g | SODIUM: 595mg | FIBER: 1g | CARBOHYDRATES: 12g | SUGAR: 3g

Beef and Pork Meatballs

When you mix these meats together, an elevated level of flavor results. Add these meatballs to some warmed marinara over pasta or rice, serve them as is, or put them in a top-split bun and serve meatball hoagies on game day. No matter how you serve them, they're sure to please.

Hands-On Time: 10 minutes
Cook Time: 16 minutes
Preheat Temperature: 350°F
Preheat Time: 3 minutes
Accessories/Prep: Fryer basket lined with parchment paper; add 1 tablespoon water below basket

Serves 4

1 slice white bread, torn into bite-sized pieces
2 tablespoons whole milk
1/2 pound ground beef
1/2 pound ground pork
1 large egg, whisked
2 tablespoons grated yellow onion
1 teaspoon Italian seasoning

WHAT TO DO WITH BREAD ENDS
When using a loaf of bread, most of us skip the ends and go straight for the middle slices. If you have a "no waste" policy in your kitchen, save these ends to use in meatballs or meatloaf.

1 In a large bowl, combine bread with milk. Add remaining ingredients and, using your hands, squeeze mixture together until fully combined.

2 Form mixture into twenty meatballs, a little less than 2 tablespoons each. Place ten meatballs in prepared fryer basket and cook 6 minutes. Flip meatballs and cook an additional 2 minutes.

3 Transfer meatballs to a large serving dish. Repeat with remaining meatballs and serve warm.

PER SERVING

CALORIES: 258 | FAT: 14g | PROTEIN: 24g | SODIUM: 126mg | FIBER: 0g | CARBOHYDRATES: 5g | SUGAR: 1g

Peachy Pork Chops

Fruit pairs perfectly with pork chops, and this recipe won't let you down. The air fryer sears all sides of the meat while keeping the inside juicy! It's simply beautiful served with some mashed potatoes and asparagus.

Hands-On Time: 5 minutes
Cook Time: 46 minutes
Preheat Temperature: 350°F
Preheat Time: 3 minutes
Accessories/Prep: Fryer basket lined with parchment paper; add 1 tablespoon water below basket

Serves 2

- 2 tablespoons peach preserves
- 1 tablespoon ketchup
- 1 tablespoon Dijon mustard
- 2 teaspoons packed light brown sugar
- 1 teaspoon Worcestershire sauce
- 1 tablespoon lime juice
- 1 tablespoon olive oil
- 2 medium cloves garlic, peeled and minced
- 2 (1"-thick) bone-in pork chops (about 10 ounces)

1 In a gallon-sized resealable plastic bag, combine preserves, ketchup, mustard, brown sugar, Worcestershire sauce, lime juice, oil, and garlic. Add pork chops and seal bag. Toss and massage mixture into pork to coat. Refrigerate 30 minutes up to overnight. Drain pork chops; discard marinade.

2 Place pork chops in prepared fryer basket. Cook 8 minutes. Flip chops and cook an additional 8 minutes. Check pork using a meat thermometer to ensure internal temperature is at least 145°F.

3 Transfer pork to a cutting board and let rest 5 minutes. Serve warm.

PER PORK CHOP

CALORIES: 238 | FAT: 5g | PROTEIN: 36g | SODIUM: 257mg | FIBER: 0g | CARBOHYDRATES: 11g | SUGAR: 8g

Sesame-Orange Crispy Pork

Shake up your weeknight with this sweet and savory dish. By thinly slicing the pork prior to cooking, you allow the air fryer to give this succulent meat crispy edges, which adds another dimension of flavor and texture to this simple dish.

Hands-On Time: 10 minutes
Cook Time: 47 minutes
Preheat Temperature: 350°F
Preheat Time: 3 minutes
Accessories/Prep: Fryer basket sprayed with olive oil cooking spray; add 2 tablespoons water below basket

Serves 4

- 1/2 cup freshly squeezed orange juice
- 2 tablespoons orange marmalade
- 1 tablespoon sesame oil
- 1 tablespoon soy sauce
- 2 teaspoons sriracha
- 1 teaspoon yellow mustard
- 1 (1-pound) pork shoulder, trimmed and thinly sliced into 1" strips
- 4 cups cooked white rice
- 1/4 cup chopped fresh cilantro
- 1 tablespoon toasted sesame seeds

1 In a medium bowl, whisk together orange juice, marmalade, oil, soy sauce, sriracha, and mustard. Set aside half of marinade. Add pork strips to bowl with remaining half of marinade and toss to coat. Refrigerate covered 30 minutes up to overnight. Drain pork; discard marinade.

2 Place pork in prepared fryer basket and cook 5 minutes. Shake basket, then cook an additional 6 minutes. Shake basket once more and cook a final 6 minutes.

3 Transfer pork to a medium bowl and toss with remaining reserved marinade. Serve over cooked rice and garnish with cilantro and sesame seeds.

PER SERVING

CALORIES: 492 | FAT: 13g | PROTEIN: 28g | SODIUM: 241mg | FIBER: 1g | CARBOHYDRATES: 60g | SUGAR: 5g

Garlic Butter Pork Chops

This traditional meal can be delivered in minutes with very simple ingredients you may already have on hand. Serve these pork chops with a potato side of your choice and a scoop of applesauce for a well-rounded meal.

Hands-On Time: 5 minutes
Cook Time: 12 minutes
Preheat Temperature: 350°F
Preheat Time: 3 minutes
Accessories/Prep: Fryer basket lined with parchment paper

Serves 2

2 (1"-thick) bone-in pork chops (about 5 ounces each)
1/2 teaspoon salt
1/4 teaspoon ground black pepper
2 tablespoons unsalted butter
1 teaspoon minced garlic
2 sprigs fresh thyme

1 Season pork chops with salt and pepper.

2 Place pork in prepared fryer basket. Cook 6 minutes. Flip and cook an additional 5 minutes. Flip again and top each pork chop with 1 tablespoon butter. Add minced garlic and a sprig of thyme to each. Cook a final 1 minute. Check pork using a meat thermometer to ensure internal temperature is at least 145°F.

3 Transfer pork to a cutting board and let rest 5 minutes. Serve warm.

PER PORK CHOP

CALORIES: 294 | FAT: 16g | PROTEIN: 36g | SODIUM: 689mg | FIBER: 0g | CARBOHYDRATES: 1g | SUGAR: 0g

Carolina Country-Style Pork Ribs

Interestingly, country-style pork ribs aren't actually cut from the ribs. They come from the end of the pork shoulder, which is also referred to as the pork butt! Regardless, these "ribs" are a boneless, fatty cut that are very tender and worth a try.

Hands-On Time: 10 minutes
Cook Time: 1 hour 10 minutes
Preheat Temperature: 350°F
Preheat Time: 3 minutes
Accessories/Prep: Fryer basket sprayed with olive oil cooking spray; add 1 tablespoon water below basket

Serves 4

1¼ cups Carolina barbecue sauce, divided
2 pounds country-style pork ribs

WHAT IS CAROLINA BARBECUE SAUCE?
You can purchase this kind of sauce bottled in the condiment aisle of your grocery store. Carolina sauce is generally a thin, vinegar-based sauce. It is tangy and delicious, but don't tell the rivals this—Kansas City, Memphis, and Texas may have something to say about it!

1 In a gallon-sized resealable plastic bag, combine 1 cup barbecue sauce and ribs. Seal bag and toss to coat. Refrigerate 30 minutes up to overnight. Drain ribs; discard marinade.

2 Place ribs in prepared fryer basket. Cook 20 minutes. Flip ribs and brush with remaining ¼ cup sauce. Cook an additional 20 minutes.

3 Transfer ribs to a plate and serve warm.

PER SERVING

CALORIES: 426 | FAT: 25g | PROTEIN: 36g | SODIUM: 126mg | FIBER: 0g | CARBOHYDRATES: 6g | SUGAR: 6g

Beer Brats and Sauerkraut

This German classic begs to be served with your favorite potato dish. The air fryer gives the sauerkraut a delicious little crunch around the edges. You can also substitute the beer in this recipe for an equal amount of beef broth and ⅛ teaspoon Worcestershire sauce. It will be just as tasty!

Hands-On Time: 10 minutes
Cook Time: 21 minutes
Preheat Temperature: 400°F
Preheat Time: 3 minutes
Accessories/Prep: Fryer basket lined with parchment paper

Serves 5

1 pound (about 5 links) uncooked pork bratwurst, pierced with a fork
1 (12-ounce) bottle lager beer
2 cups water
½ medium yellow onion, peeled and sliced into half-moons
2 cups drained sauerkraut
2 tablespoons German mustard

BRATWURST TIME-SAVING HACK!
Use precooked bratwurst and skip step one of this recipe. No boiling is necessary. Just add links to fryer basket and cook until warmed through, approximately 5 minutes.

1 In a medium saucepan over high heat, combine bratwurst with beer, water, and onion. Bring to a boil. Reduce heat to medium and simmer 15 minutes. Drain.

2 Place bratwurst and onion in prepared fryer basket. Cook 3 minutes, then flip bratwurst. Add sauerkraut and cook an additional 3 minutes. Check bratwurst using a meat thermometer to ensure internal temperature is at least 160°F.

3 Transfer bratwurst, onion, and sauerkraut to a large plate and serve warm with mustard on the side.

PER SERVING

CALORIES: 311 | FAT: 24g | PROTEIN: 13g | SODIUM: 1,244mg | FIBER: 2g | CARBOHYDRATES: 6g | SUGAR: 1g

Cubano Tortilla Wraps

Do you have some leftover barbecued pulled pork shoulder? This twist on the classic Cubano sandwich is the solution. The crisp air fryer tortilla mimics the traditional bread made crunchy by the panini press.

Hands-On Time: 15 minutes
Cook Time: 4 minutes
Preheat Temperature: 350°F
Preheat Time: 3 minutes
Accessories/Prep: Fryer basket lined with aluminum foil

Serves 4

4 (8") flour tortillas
1 cup cooked pulled pork
1/2 cup shredded Swiss cheese
4 ounces deli ham, chopped
4 teaspoons yellow mustard
12 dill pickle slices

1 Place 1 tortilla on a cutting surface. Using a sharp knife, make a cut from the center of the tortilla to the edge. Imagine dividing the tortilla into four sections with the cut facing toward you. To the bottom left quadrant, add 1/4 cup pulled pork. To the top left quadrant, add 2 tablespoons Swiss. To the upper right quadrant, add 1 ounce ham. To the bottom right quadrant, add 1 teaspoon mustard and 3 pickle slices.

2 Fold tortilla as follows to form a triangle: Begin by folding the bottom left quadrant over the top left quadrant; then, proceeding clockwise, fold this triangle over the top right quadrant and finally down over the bottom right quadrant. Repeat with remaining tortillas.

3 Place wraps in prepared fryer basket and cook 2 minutes. Flip wraps, then cook an additional 2 minutes. Transfer to a plate and serve warm

PER WRAP

CALORIES: 360 | FAT: 11g | PROTEIN: 21g | SODIUM: 1,999mg | FIBER: 4g | CARBOHYDRATES: 41g | SUGAR: 12g

Pork Banh Mi-Inspired Bowls

This bowl mimics the flavors of a typical banh mi in a different format. It's a recipe that you'll want to make over and over again!

Hands-On Time: 15 minutes
Cook Time: 16 minutes
Preheat Temperature: 350°F
Preheat Time: 3 minutes
Accessories/Prep: Fryer basket sprayed with olive oil cooking spray; add 1 tablespoon water below basket

Serves 4

Crema
1/4 cup sour cream
1/4 cup mayonnaise
1 tablespoon lime juice
1/2 teaspoon salt

Vegetables
4 medium radishes, julienned
1 medium shallot, peeled and thinly sliced
3 tablespoons rice vinegar
2 tablespoons water
1/8 teaspoon salt
2 medium carrots, peeled and grated
4 cups shredded napa cabbage
1/4 cup chopped fresh basil

Pork
1 tablespoon sesame oil
1 tablespoon soy sauce
2 teaspoons sriracha
2 teaspoons honey
1 (1") piece fresh ginger, peeled and minced
1 (1-pound) pork shoulder, trimmed and sliced into 1" strips

1 In a small bowl, whisk together Crema ingredients. In a separate large bowl, combine radishes, shallot, vinegar, water, salt, carrots, cabbage, and basil. Cover and refrigerate Crema and Vegetables separately for 30 minutes up to overnight while preparing pork.

2 To prepare Pork, in a separate large bowl, whisk together oil, soy sauce, sriracha, honey, and ginger. Set aside half of marinade. Add pork strips to bowl with remaining marinade and toss to coat. Refrigerate covered until ready to use. Drain pork; discard marinade.

3 Place pork in prepared fryer basket and cook 8 minutes. Toss, then cook an additional 8 minutes. Transfer pork to bowl with reserved marinade and toss. Divide Vegetables evenly among four bowls. Top with Pork and drizzle with Crema. Serve immediately.

PER SERVING

CALORIES: 327 | FAT: 20g | PROTEIN: 25g | SODIUM: 605mg | FIBER: 3g | CARBOHYDRATES: 9g | SUGAR: 5g

Pork and Mushroom Meatzza

For the carb-conscious people who love pizza, the Meatzza is your new friend. Using the pork as the crust and then adding some sauce, mozzarella, and your favorite toppings, you can once again enjoy this takeout delight!

Hands-On Time: 15 minutes
Cook Time: 11 minutes
Preheat Temperature: 350°F
Preheat Time: 3 minutes
Accessories/Prep: Fryer basket and pizza pan

Serves 4

- 1/2 pound Italian pork sausage, removed from casings
- 2 tablespoons pizza sauce
- 1 teaspoon dried basil
- 1/4 cup sliced mushrooms
- 1/2 cup shredded part-skim mozzarella cheese

1 Press pork sausage evenly in pizza pan and up the sides. Place in fryer basket and cook 7 minutes. Remove from basket and drain oil. The meat will separate from the sides a bit.

2 Spread pizza sauce over the "crust" up to 1/2" from the edge. Sprinkle basil over sauce. Add mushrooms and then cover with mozzarella. Cook an additional 4 minutes.

3 Remove pizza pan and let cool 5 minutes. Slice and serve warm.

PER SERVING

CALORIES: 189 | FAT: 12g | PROTEIN: 15g | SODIUM: 496mg | FIBER: 0g | CARBOHYDRATES: 2g | SUGAR: 1g

7

Fish and Seafood Main Dishes

Complete with omega-3 fatty acids, protein, and B vitamins, seafood is both delicious and nutritious, but it can be intimidating to cook at home. Whether it's due to fear of over- or undercooking, or simply lack of experience, seafood is generally something people steer away from. Luckily, with the air fryer, you'll have quick, easy, impressive dishes on your table in a matter of minutes.

Or let's say you're a more adventurous cook who already prepares seafood dishes at home. Go ahead and try out these air fryer recipes instead of your tried-and-true options. The convection heat component offers a new way to cook it, providing different textures and flavors. So don't be afraid to switch it up. Plus, you don't need to worry about the skin getting stuck to the pan or smelling up the entire house like you might when cooking in the oven!

High in nutrients and low in calories, fish and shellfish dishes are no-brainer additions to your weekly meal plan. From Barbecued Salmon Fillets and Lobsta Cobb Salad to After-School Fish Sticks and Fried Butterflied Shrimp, these recipes will be delicious inclusions to your go-to menu.

Barbecued Salmon Fillets

So you're having a backyard barbecue, and there are those one or two guests who don't eat red meat. No worries! The same barbecue sauce you're slathering on the ribs will pair very nicely with some salmon fillets.

Hands-On Time: 5 minutes
Cook Time: 7 minutes
Preheat Temperature: 375°F
Preheat Time: 3 minutes
Accessories/Prep: Fryer basket lined with parchment paper

Serves 2

2 (6-ounce) boneless salmon fillets, about 1" thick
¼ cup barbecue sauce

1 On a cutting board, rub barbecue sauce over salmon fillets.

2 Place salmon skin side up in prepared fryer basket. Cook 7 minutes.

3 Serve warm.

PER SERVING

CALORIES: 277 | FAT: 9g | PROTEIN: 31g | SODIUM: 433mg | FIBER: 0g | CARBOHYDRATES: 15g | SUGAR: 12g

Lemon Butter Salmon Fillets

Salmon is a powerhouse meal filled with nutrients, good fats, and flavor. Add it to the menu at least two or three times a week for dinner or lunch to pack in those omega-3 fatty acids.

Hands-On Time: 5 minutes
Cook Time: 7 minutes
Preheat Temperature: 375°F
Preheat Time: 3 minutes
Accessories/Prep: Fryer basket lined with parchment paper

Serves 2

2 (6-ounce) boneless salmon fillets, about 1" thick
2 tablespoons unsalted butter, melted
½ teaspoon garlic salt
4 lemon slices

1 Place salmon fillets skin side up in prepared fryer basket. Cook 5 minutes.

2 Flip salmon. Brush fillets with butter, sprinkle with garlic salt, and place 2 lemon slices on each fillet. Cook an additional 2 minutes.

3 Transfer salmon to plates and serve warm.

PER SERVING

CALORIES: 318 | FAT: 19g | PROTEIN: 30g | SODIUM: 558mg | FIBER: 0g | CARBOHYDRATES: 0g | SUGAR: 0g

Salmon Patties with Dill Sauce

This recipe calls for canned salmon to make things easier, but leftover cooked salmon or freshly cooked salmon flaked into pieces are perfect substitutes when preparing these omega-3-filled powerhouse patties.

Hands-On Time: 15 minutes
Cook Time: 20 minutes
Preheat Temperature: 400°F
Preheat Time: 3 minutes
Accessories/Prep: Fryer basket lined with parchment paper

Serves 4

Dill Sauce

1/4 cup sour cream
2 tablespoons mayonnaise
2 medium cloves garlic, peeled and minced
2 tablespoons chopped fresh dill
2 teaspoons lime juice
1/4 teaspoon salt

Salmon Patties

1 (14.75-ounce) can salmon, drained
1/2 cup mayonnaise
1 large egg, whisked
2 tablespoons finely minced red bell pepper
1/8 teaspoon salt
1/2 cup panko bread crumbs, divided
Olive oil cooking spray

1 In a small bowl, whisk together Dill Sauce ingredients. Refrigerate covered overnight up to 3 days.

2 In a medium bowl, combine salmon, mayonnaise, egg, bell pepper, salt, and 1/4 cup bread crumbs. Form mixture into eight patties. Roll patties in remaining bread crumbs.

3 Place four patties in prepared fryer basket. Spray tops of patties with cooking spray. Cook 5 minutes. Flip patties and spray again. Cook an additional 5 minutes. Transfer patties to a large serving dish. Repeat with remaining patties. Let rest 5 minutes before serving warm with Dill Sauce on the side.

PER SERVING

CALORIES: 430 | FAT: 32g | PROTEIN: 20g | SODIUM: 726mg | FIBER: 0g | CARBOHYDRATES: 12g | SUGAR: 1g

Lobsta Cobb Salad

Forget the sad, boring salads of the past. This special dish will have you reaching for salad again and again! If you're looking to really indulge, don't forget the artisanal bread and chilled rosé to go with it.

Hands-On Time: 10 minutes
Cook Time: 8 minutes
Preheat Temperature: 400°F
Preheat Time: 3 minutes
Accessories/Prep: Fryer basket lined with parchment paper

Serves 2

2 (5-ounce) frozen uncooked lobster tails, thawed
1 tablespoon unsalted butter, melted
3 cups mixed greens
1/4 cup red wine vinaigrette
2 large eggs, hard-boiled, peeled, and halved
2 slices bacon, cooked and crumbled
2 medium Roma tomatoes, seeded and diced
1/4 cup crumbled blue cheese
1 medium avocado, peeled, pitted, and sliced

1 Using kitchen shears, cut down the middle of the lobster tails on the softer side. Carefully run your finger between the lobster meat and the shell to loosen meat.

2 Place tails cut side up in prepared fryer basket. Cook 4 minutes. Brush with butter and cook an additional 4 minutes. Transfer tails to a cutting board and let sit until cool enough to handle. Remove meat from shells. Dice lobster meat into 1" bites.

3 Divide greens between two bowls and toss with vinaigrette. Top with remaining ingredients for a decorative presentation. Serve.

PER SERVING

CALORIES: 527 | FAT: 36g | PROTEIN: 30g | SODIUM: 1,170mg | FIBER: 6g | CARBOHYDRATES: 14g | SUGAR: 5g

Crab Cakes

Take a staycation to Baltimore's Inner Harbor with these delicate, healthy Crab Cakes. To take this dish up a notch, serve with asparagus and a hollandaise sauce. Alternately, the Blistered Tomatoes from Chapter 4 would pair well with this dish.

Hands-On Time: 15 minutes
Cook Time: 10 minutes
Preheat Temperature: 400°F
Preheat Time: 3 minutes
Accessories/Prep: Fryer basket lined with parchment paper

1 In a medium bowl, combine all ingredients. Form into four patties.

2 Place patties in prepared fryer basket. Cook 5 minutes. Gently flip crab cakes. Cook an additional 5 minutes.

3 Transfer to a plate and serve warm.

Serves 2

8 ounces uncooked lump crabmeat, picked over and any shells discarded
2 tablespoons mayonnaise
$1/2$ teaspoon Dijon mustard
$1/2$ teaspoon lemon juice
2 teaspoons grated yellow onion
$1/4$ teaspoon prepared horseradish
4 saltine crackers, crushed
1 large egg white, whisked
$1/2$ teaspoon Old Bay seasoning

PER SERVING

CALORIES: 226 | FAT: 11g | PROTEIN: 23g | SODIUM: 987mg | FIBER: 0g | CARBOHYDRATES: 6g | SUGAR: 0g

QUICK AND EASY BLENDER HOLLANDAISE
Combine 2 egg yolks, pinch salt, pinch cayenne pepper, and 1 tablespoon lemon juice. While blending at high speed, slowly drizzle in ¼ cup melted butter until a thick sauce forms. Taste. Add extra salt and/or lemon juice if necessary.

Tuna Croquettes

This is a crunchy treat that is relatively inexpensive, yet has a fancy feel! Croquettes are usually breaded and deep-fried, making them delicious yet not exactly the healthiest. In this case, however, the air fryer steps in to give the croquettes the crispiness that makes them what they are and saves the grease.

Hands-On Time: 10 minutes
Cook Time: 22 minutes
Preheat Temperature: 350°F
Preheat Time: 3 minutes
Accessories/Prep: Fryer basket lined with parchment paper

Serves 4

3 (5-ounce) cans white tuna in water, drained
1/3 cup mayonnaise
2 tablespoons minced celery
2 teaspoons dried dill
1 teaspoon lime juice
1 large egg, whisked
1/4 teaspoon salt
1/2 teaspoon ground black pepper
1 cup panko bread crumbs

1 In a large bowl, combine tuna, mayonnaise, celery, dill, lime juice, egg, salt, and pepper.

2 Form into sixteen balls, about 2 tablespoons each. Roll each ball in bread crumbs, covering all sides.

3 Place eight croquettes in prepared fryer basket. Cook 6 minutes. Flip croquettes and cook an additional 5 minutes. Transfer to a plate. Repeat with remaining croquettes. Serve warm.

PER SERVING

CALORIES: 317 | FAT: 16g | PROTEIN: 21g | SODIUM: 548mg | FIBER: 0g | CARBOHYDRATES: 21g | SUGAR: 1g

Herbed Pecan-Crusted Steelhead Trout

The combination of pecans and trout is a powerhouse duo! The nutritional value of this meal ups the ante, and the ease of cooking fish in the air fryer ensures that you'll be cooking fish more often at home.

Hands-On Time: 10 minutes
Cook Time: 9 minutes
Preheat Temperature: 350°F
Preheat Time: 3 minutes
Accessories/Prep: Fryer basket lined with parchment paper

Serves 2

2 (5-ounce) boneless steelhead trout fillets, about 1" thick
1 tablespoon Dijon mustard
2 tablespoons Italian-style bread crumbs
1 tablespoon pecan pieces
2 tablespoons salted butter, melted

1 On a cutting board, pat fillets dry with a paper towel, skin side down. Rub tops with mustard.

2 In a small bowl, combine bread crumbs, pecan pieces, and melted butter. Press mixture onto the top sides of fillets.

3 Place fillets in prepared fryer basket and cook 9 minutes. Remove from basket and serve warm.

PER FILLET

CALORIES: 378 | FAT: 22g | PROTEIN: 32g | SODIUM: 362mg | FIBER: 1g | CARBOHYDRATES: 6g | SUGAR: 1g

THE DIFFERENCE BETWEEN TROUT AND STEELHEAD TROUT

Although the same species, trout is strictly a freshwater fish, whereas a steelhead spends some time in the ocean. Also, steelhead trout is considered even healthier than salmon, containing more omega-3 acids.

Salt and Vinegar–Crusted Cod

Dressing fish and chips with malt vinegar is an English tradition. Using crushed salt and vinegar potato chips recalls the flavor of that delicious street food. And if you like this method, use your imagination and try other varieties of potato chips.

Hands-On Time: 10 minutes
Cook Time: 10 minutes
Preheat Temperature: 350°F
Preheat Time: 3 minutes
Accessories/Prep: Fryer basket lined with parchment paper

Serves 2

- ½ cup crushed salt and vinegar potato chips
- 1 teaspoon lemon juice
- 1 tablespoon unsalted butter, melted
- 2 (6-ounce) boneless, skinless cod fillets

1 In a small bowl, combine potato chips, lemon juice, and butter. Press potato chip mixture evenly across tops of fillets.

2 Place fish in prepared fryer basket. Cook 10 minutes until fish is opaque and flakes easily with a fork.

3 Transfer fish to serving plates and serve warm.

PER FILLET

CALORIES: 280 | FAT: 11g | PROTEIN: 33g | SODIUM: 190mg | FIBER: 0g | CARBOHYDRATES: 8g | SUGAR: 0g

KICKIN' KOLESLAW

For a quick and flavorful coleslaw to accompany this fish, combine the following ingredients and refrigerate until ready to use: 12-ounce bag coleslaw mix, ¼ cup mayonnaise, 1 teaspoon Dijon mustard, 1 teaspoon lemon zest, 1 tablespoon lemon juice, and ¼ teaspoon salt. And if you are feeling a little spicy, add some prepared horseradish or hot sauce!

Mediterranean-Style Sea Bass

This dish is flaky, succulent, and sexy. Sea bass is a major upgrade to a basic cod dish, which makes this a special-occasion meal. The silky olive oil, the sharpness of the olives, the cooling of the tomatoes, and the saltiness of the capers all come together to make this a winner!

Hands-On Time: 10 minutes
Cook Time: 7 minutes
Preheat Temperature: 350°F
Preheat Time: 3 minutes
Accessories/Prep: Fryer basket; cake barrel sprayed with cooking spray

Serves 2

2 (6-ounce) boneless sea bass fillets, about 1" thick
2 teaspoons olive oil
¼ teaspoon garlic salt
⅛ teaspoon cayenne pepper
¼ cup pitted and quartered kalamata olives
12 cherry tomatoes, halved
1 tablespoon drained capers

1   On a cutting board, pat fillets dry with a paper towel, skin side down. Brush fillets with oil and place in prepared cake barrel. Season with garlic salt and cayenne.

2   Arrange olives, tomatoes, and capers around fish fillets. Add barrel to fryer basket and cook 7 minutes. Remove barrel from basket.

3   Transfer fish and vegetables to plates. Serve warm.

PER FILLET

CALORIES: 258 | FAT: 11g | PROTEIN: 32g | SODIUM: 698mg | FIBER: 2g | CARBOHYDRATES: 4g | SUGAR: 3g

After-School Fish Sticks

If your kiddos like fish sticks, but you want to be in charge of the ingredients, make your own! But don't worry—you don't need kids (or school) in order to enjoy these. They make for a great snack or dinner anytime.

Hands-On Time: 10 minutes
Cook Time: 20 minutes
Preheat Temperature: 350°F
Preheat Time: 3 minutes
Accessories/Prep: Fryer basket lined with parchment paper

Serves 4

1 pound boneless cod fillets, cut into 1" sticks
¼ cup all-purpose flour
2 tablespoons cornstarch
½ teaspoon salt
¼ teaspoon ground black pepper
1 large egg
1 tablespoon water
1 cup plain bread crumbs

1 On a cutting board, pat fish dry with paper towels. In a medium bowl, combine flour, cornstarch, salt, and pepper. In a separate medium bowl, whisk together egg and water. Add bread crumbs to a third medium bowl.

2 Dredge 1 fish stick in flour mixture. Shake off excess flour, then dip fish in whisked egg. Shake off excess egg and roll in bread crumbs. Shake off excess bread crumbs. Transfer to a plate and repeat with remaining fish sticks.

3 Place half of fish sticks in prepared fryer basket. Cook 5 minutes. Carefully flip fish sticks and cook an additional 5 minutes. Transfer fish sticks to a serving plate. Repeat with remaining fish and serve warm.

PER SERVING

CALORIES: 219 | FAT: 2g | PROTEIN: 22g | SODIUM: 800mg | FIBER: 1g | CARBOHYDRATES: 24g | SUGAR: 1g

Beer-Battered Oysters

Whether you eat these with some fries or make a po'boy sammie, fried oysters are delicious, especially when you know that they aren't deep-fried in day-old oil in the back of an ocean bar. Your air fryer will ensure these have that crispy and fresh outer layer you're looking for.

Hands-On Time: 10 minutes
Cook Time: 16 minutes
Preheat Temperature: 400°F
Preheat Time: 3 minutes
Accessories/Prep: Fryer basket lined with parchment paper

Serves 4

16 ounces uncooked shucked oysters
1 large egg
1 cup lager
2 teaspoons hot sauce
¼ cup cornstarch
¼ cup all-purpose flour
1 cup panko bread crumbs
½ teaspoon salt

HOMEMADE TARTAR SAUCE

To make your own tartar sauce, combine the following ingredients: ½ cup mayonnaise, 1 tablespoon Dijon mustard, 2 tablespoons small-diced sweet pickle relish, ⅛ teaspoon salt, and ¼ teaspoon black pepper. To kick it up a notch, substitute 2 tablespoons drained jarred diced jalapeño peppers (or even more if you like the heat) for the pickle relish.

1   Rinse and drain oysters. Pat dry with a paper towel and set aside. In a small bowl, whisk together egg, lager, and hot sauce. In a second small bowl, combine cornstarch, flour, bread crumbs, and salt.

2   Dip 1 oyster in egg mixture. Shake off excess egg, then dredge in bread crumb mixture. Shake off excess bread crumbs. Transfer to a plate and repeat with remaining oysters. Place half of oysters in prepared fryer basket and cook 4 minutes. Carefully flip oysters. Cook an additional 4 minutes.

3   Transfer oysters to a serving plate. Repeat with remaining oysters and serve warm.

PER SERVING

CALORIES: 210 | FAT: 3g | PROTEIN: 14g | SODIUM: 499mg | FIBER: 0g | CARBOHYDRATES: 28g | SUGAR: 1g

Spicy Fried Sardines

Sardines are affordable and low in mercury and other metals. Plus, breading them and cooking them in the air fryer gives them a more appealing appearance.

Hands-On Time: 5 minutes
Cook Time: 6 minutes
Preheat Temperature: 350°F
Preheat Time: 3 minutes
Accessories/Prep: Fryer basket lined with parchment paper

Serves 2

1/2 cup panko bread crumbs
2 (3.75-ounce) cans boneless, skinless sardines in hot sauce
2 lemon wedges

1 Place bread crumbs in a shallow dish. Roll sardines in dish to coat.

2 Place breaded sardines in prepared fryer basket. Cook 3 minutes. Gently flip sardines. Cook an additional 3 minutes.

3 Transfer sardines to a large serving dish and serve warm with lemon wedges.

PER SERVING

CALORIES: 100 | FAT: 5g | PROTEIN: 24g | SODIUM: 405mg | FIBER: 0g | CARBOHYDRATES: 23g | SUGAR: 1g

Buttery Sea Scallops

These scallops would be great over pasta, with vegetables and rice, or on their own. The air-fryer perfectly sears the scallops on all sides, so you can enjoy them however you please.

Hands-On Time: 5 minutes
Cook Time: 6 minutes
Preheat Temperature: 400°F
Preheat Time: 3 minutes
Accessories/Prep: Fryer basket lined with parchment paper

Serves 2

1 pound (about 10) uncooked jumbo sea scallops
2 tablespoons unsalted butter, melted, divided
2 tablespoons chopped fresh parsley
1/8 teaspoon salt

1 In a medium bowl, combine scallops with 1 tablespoon butter. Toss to coat all sides.

2 Place scallops in prepared fryer basket. Cook 3 minutes. Flip scallops. Brush tops of scallops with remaining butter. Cook an additional 3 minutes.

3 Transfer scallops to plates. Garnish with parsley and salt. Serve warm.

PER SERVING

CALORIES: 258 | FAT: 11g | PROTEIN: 28g | SODIUM: 1,037mg | FIBER: 0g | CARBOHYDRATES: 7g | SUGAR: 0g

Shrimpy Jalapeño Poppers

Shrimp cooks quickly, and wrapping them in prosciutto instead of bacon lends a salty, fatty flavor without adding the extra cooking time needed for bacon. Stuffed with two kinds of cheeses and given a little kick from the jalapeños, this shrimp recipe will be a favorite!

Hands-On Time: 10 minutes
Cook Time: 18 minutes
Preheat Temperature: 400°F
Preheat Time: 3 minutes
Accessories/Prep: Fryer basket lined with parchment paper

Serves 4

- 3 tablespoons cream cheese, room temperature
- 2 tablespoons finely shredded Cheddar cheese
- 2 tablespoons drained jarred diced jalapeño peppers
- 1 tablespoon mayonnaise
- ¼ teaspoon ground black pepper
- 20 uncooked large tail-on shrimp, shelled, deveined, and sliced down the spine
- 10 ounces prosciutto, cut into 20 slices
- ¼ cup chopped fresh parsley

1 In a medium bowl, combine cream cheese, Cheddar, jalapeños, mayonnaise, and black pepper. Evenly press cream cheese mixture into cut spine of shrimp. Wrap 1 piece prosciutto around each shrimp to hold in cream cheese mixture.

2 Place ten prepared shrimp in prepared fryer basket. Cook 5 minutes. Flip shrimp. Cook an additional 4 minutes.

3 Transfer cooked shrimp to a large serving plate. Repeat with remaining shrimp. Garnish with chopped parsley and serve warm.

PER SERVING

CALORIES: 316 | FAT: 23g | PROTEIN: 23g | SODIUM: 673mg | FIBER: 0g | CARBOHYDRATES: 3g | SUGAR: 0g

Scallop Bowls with Spring Greens and Quinoa

Scallops can be tricky to get right when cooked on the stovetop, but in the air fryer it's guaranteed they'll be perfectly cooked and crisped. Add them to these bowls with oranges, walnuts, quinoa, and greens, and you'll have a flavor-packed yet healthy meal.

Hands-On Time: 15 minutes
Cook Time: 6 minutes
Preheat Temperature: 400°F
Preheat Time: 3 minutes
Accessories/Prep: Fryer basket lined with parchment paper

Serves 4

3 tablespoons olive oil
1 tablespoon white wine vinegar
1 teaspoon Dijon mustard
2 medium cloves garlic, peeled and minced
12 uncooked jumbo sea scallops (about 8 ounces)
1 tablespoon unsalted butter, melted
1 cup cooked quinoa
4 cups spring greens
1/2 cup walnut pieces
1 (11-ounce) can mandarin oranges, drained

1 In a small bowl, whisk together oil, vinegar, mustard, and garlic. Refrigerate covered for 30 minutes up to overnight.

2 Place scallops in prepared fryer basket. Cook 3 minutes. Flip scallops. Brush with melted butter. Cook an additional 3 minutes.

3 Divide quinoa evenly among four bowls. Toss greens with dressing and evenly add on top of quinoa along with scallops, walnut pieces, and oranges. Serve immediately.

PER SERVING

CALORIES: 387 | **FAT:** 28g | **PROTEIN:** 12g | **SODIUM:** 283mg | **FIBER:** 4g | **CARBOHYDRATES:** 21g | **SUGAR:** 6g

Fried Butterflied Shrimp

Butterflying shrimp helps you cook them quicker and more evenly. It also presents beautifully with not much extra work. Serve these gems up with some cocktail sauce and enjoy!

Hands-On Time: 10 minutes
Cook Time: 6 minutes
Preheat Temperature: 380°F
Preheat Time: 3 minutes
Accessories/Prep: Fryer basket lined with parchment paper

Serves 2

⅓ cup all-purpose flour
½ teaspoon salt
1 large egg
2 tablespoons whole milk
¼ cup cornmeal
¼ cup panko bread crumbs
½ pound uncooked medium shrimp, shelled, deveined, and butterflied

WHAT DOES "BUTTERFLIED" MEAN?

Deveining shrimp is cutting a shallow line down the spine of the shrimp and cleaning out the vein. To butterfly the shrimp, simply make a deeper cut in the same spot, ensuring that the knife doesn't cut all the way through. Essentially, you are creating two wings on the shrimp, as if it were a butterfly.

1 In a small bowl, combine flour and salt. In a second small bowl, whisk together egg and milk. In a third small bowl, combine cornmeal and bread crumbs.

2 Dredge 1 shrimp in flour mixture. Shake off excess flour, then dip in egg mixture. Shake off excess egg and roll in bread crumb mixture. Shake off excess bread crumbs. Transfer to a plate and repeat with remaining shrimp.

3 Place shrimp in prepared fryer basket. Cook 3 minutes. Gently flip shrimp. Cook an additional 3 minutes. Transfer shrimp to a plate and serve warm.

PER SERVING

CALORIES: 226 | FAT: 4g | PROTEIN: 19g | SODIUM: 976mg | FIBER: 1g | CARBOHYDRATES: 28g | SUGAR: 1g

Lemon Butter Shrimp

Shrimp are not only high in protein, but they are also low in calories and delicious. Although they're perfect served as a main course, you may want to try to them served over some pappardelle or a delicious risotto.

Hands-On Time: 5 minutes
Cook Time: 6 minutes
Preheat Temperature: 350°F
Preheat Time: 3 minutes
Accessories/Prep: Fryer basket

Serves 2

2 tablespoons unsalted butter, melted
1 tablespoon lemon juice
1/4 teaspoon garlic salt
1 pound uncooked medium shrimp, shelled and deveined
1/4 cup chopped fresh parsley
2 wedges lemon

1 In a large bowl, combine butter, lemon juice, and garlic salt.

2 Toss shrimp in butter mixture to coat. Place in fryer basket and cook 3 minutes. Gently flip shrimp. Cook an additional 3 minutes.

3 Divide shrimp evenly between two bowls and garnish with parsley. Serve warm with lemon wedges.

PER SERVING

CALORIES: 240 | FAT: 12g | PROTEIN: 26g | SODIUM: 1,324mg | FIBER: 0g | CARBOHYDRATES: 3g | SUGAR: 0g

Ginger Shrimp Rangoons

This fun recipe is a fresh twist on crab rangoon, everyone's favorite addition to the takeout order. These rangoons include fresh shrimp, a kick of ginger, and the same crispiness as the deep-fried version, without any of the oil.

Hands-On Time: 30 minutes
Cook Time: 24 minutes
Preheat Temperature: 330°F
Preheat Time: 3 minutes
Accessories/Prep: Fryer basket

Serves 8

- 1/2 pound cooked medium shrimp, peeled, deveined, and finely chopped
- 8 ounces cream cheese, room temperature
- 2 medium scallions, trimmed and chopped (green and white parts included)
- 1 teaspoon finely diced fresh ginger
- 3 medium cloves garlic, peeled and minced
- 1 teaspoon soy sauce
- 1/2 teaspoon gochujang sauce
- 1/4 teaspoon salt
- 40 wonton wrappers
- Olive oil cooking spray

1 In a medium bowl, combine shrimp, cream cheese, scallions, ginger, garlic, soy sauce, gochujang sauce, and salt.

2 Place 1 wonton wrapper on a cutting board. Place 1 teaspoon shrimp mixture in middle of wrapper. Dip your finger in a water bowl and run it around the perimeter of the wonton. Bring all corners to the center and press the straight edges together. Repeat with remaining wontons and shrimp mixture.

3 Place one-third of rangoons in fryer basket. Spray tops with cooking spray and cook 8 minutes. Transfer to a plate. Repeat with remaining rangoons. Serve warm.

PER SERVING

CALORIES: 251 | FAT: 9g | PROTEIN: 12g | SODIUM: 713mg | FIBER: 1g | CARBOHYDRATES: 26g | SUGAR: 1g

Stuffed Calamari in Tomato Sauce

When most people think of calamari, they think of fried tubes. Although those are quite tasty, they're not the only way to serve up this seafood. The tubes can be stuffed with sausage and the flavorings of your choice.

Hands-On Time: 15 minutes
Cook Time: 13 minutes
Preheat Temperature: 350°F
Preheat Time: 3 minutes
Accessories/Prep: Fryer basket; cake barrel sprayed with cooking spray

Serves 2

- ¼ pound mild Italian ground sausage, cooked
- 2 tablespoons finely diced red onion
- ¼ cup plain bread crumbs
- 2 tablespoons drained jarred diced pimientos
- 1 large egg, beaten
- 4 medium calamari tubes
- ½ cup marinara sauce

1 In a medium bowl, combine cooked sausage, onion, bread crumbs, pimientos, and egg. Stuff calamari tubes with mixture. Use toothpicks to close.

2 Spread marinara in prepared cake barrel and arrange stuffed calamari over sauce. Place cake barrel in fryer basket and cook 10 minutes. Brush sauce over calamari and cook an additional 3 minutes.

3 Let cool 10 minutes. Transfer to plates. Serve warm.

PER SERVING

CALORIES: 522 | FAT: 21g | PROTEIN: 53g | SODIUM: 1,196mg | FIBER: 2g | CARBOHYDRATES: 25g | SUGAR: 6g

Oh-Boy Fish Sandwiches

Who needs deep-fried fish sandwiches from a fast-food joint when you can make your own that are fresh with tasty toppings? Try these sandwiches topped with some pickled vegetables for a satisfying and refreshing contrast to the fried fish.

Hands-On Time: 10 minutes
Cook Time: 12 minutes
Preheat Temperature: 375°F
Preheat Time: 3 minutes
Accessories/Prep: Fryer basket lined with parchment paper

Serves 4

Fish
1/3 cup all-purpose flour
2 tablespoons cornstarch
1 teaspoon smoked paprika
1 teaspoon salt
1/4 cup whole milk
1 large egg
1/2 cup panko bread crumbs
4 (6-ounce) cod fillets, cut in half

Sandwiches
2 tablespoons mayonnaise
1 large tomato, seeded and sliced
1/8 teaspoon salt
1/8 teaspoon ground black pepper
4 hamburger buns

1 In a shallow bowl, combine flour, cornstarch, paprika, and salt. In a second shallow bowl, whisk together milk and egg. In a third shallow bowl, add bread crumbs. Dredge a cod slice in flour mixture. Shake off excess flour, then dip in egg mixture. Shake off excess egg and dredge in bread crumbs. Shake off excess bread crumbs. Transfer to a plate and repeat with remaining cod.

2 Place half of cod in prepared fryer basket. Cook 3 minutes. Gently flip fish, then cook 3 additional minutes. Transfer fish to a large serving plate. Repeat with remaining fish.

3 To construct sandwiches, spread mayonnaise on each bun. Add fish and tomatoes. Sprinkle salt and pepper on top of tomatoes. Serve immediately.

PER SANDWICH

CALORIES: 420 | FAT: 9g | PROTEIN: 35g | SODIUM: 1,404mg | FIBER: 2g | CARBOHYDRATES: 46g | SUGAR: 5g

Hummus Tuna Melts on English Muffins

Hummus adds another layer of flavor to this classic open-faced sandwich. Not only does it contribute to the taste; it adds additional fiber and protein to this light meal. Whip up this quick dish for lunch or a snack to get you through the day.

Hands-On Time: 10 minutes
Cook Time: 4 minutes
Preheat Temperature: 350°F
Preheat Time: 3 minutes
Accessories/Prep: Fryer basket

Serves 2

1 (6-ounce) can white tuna in water, drained
$1/4$ cup mayonnaise
2 teaspoons yellow mustard
2 tablespoons minced celery
1 tablespoon minced yellow onion
$1/8$ teaspoon salt
$1/8$ teaspoon ground black pepper
4 tablespoons hummus
2 English muffins, split
4 slices beefsteak tomatoes, sliced $1/2"$ thick
4 (1-ounce) slices Swiss cheese

1 In a medium bowl, combine tuna, mayonnaise, mustard, celery, onion, salt, and pepper.

2 Spread 1 tablespoon hummus over each English muffin half. Divide tuna salad evenly among muffin halves. Place 1 tomato slice on each and top with Swiss.

3 Place muffin halves in fryer basket and cook 4 minutes until cheese starts to brown. Remove and serve warm.

PER SERVING

CALORIES: 654 | FAT: 39g | PROTEIN: 37g | SODIUM: 952mg | FIBER: 5g | CARBOHYDRATES: 35g | SUGAR: 4g

BUMP UP THE HUMMUS!
This Middle Eastern staple is full of not only delicious flavor but also of vitamins and minerals. Try flavors such as roasted red pepper, garlic, and even lemon twist!

Salmon Melts on French Bread

Small baguettes are sold at some specialty stores and would be a perfect size for this recipe. But if you buy a full-size baguette, it won't likely go to waste, and it does make great croutons (see the Crispy Croutons recipe in Chapter 3)!

Hands-On Time: 10 minutes
Cook Time: 4 minutes
Preheat Temperature: 350°F
Preheat Time: 3 minutes
Accessories/Prep: Fryer basket

Serves 2

1 (7.5-ounce) can sockeye salmon in water, drained
1/4 cup mayonnaise
1 tablespoon Dijon mustard
1 teaspoon lemon juice
1 tablespoon grated yellow onion
1 teaspoon dried dill
1/8 teaspoon salt
1/8 teaspoon ground black pepper
8 (1/4"-thick) slices French baguette
4 (1.4-ounce) slices Havarti cheese, halved

1. In a medium bowl, combine salmon, mayonnaise, mustard, lemon juice, onion, dill, salt, and pepper.

2. Divide salmon salad evenly among bread slices and spread. Top each with ½ slice Havarti.

3. Place open-faced sandwiches in fryer basket. Cook 4 minutes until cheese starts to brown. Remove and serve warm.

PER SERVING

CALORIES: 788 | FAT: 52g | PROTEIN: 51g | SODIUM: 1,714mg | FIBER: 1g | CARBOHYDRATES: 31g | SUGAR: 3g

8

Vegetarian Dishes

Whether you are a vegetarian, hard-core vegan, or just someone interested in Meatless Mondays and reducing the amount of animal protein that you're consuming, this chapter has you covered. As you make your way through these recipes, keep in mind that some include cheese alternatives and some don't, because cheese is acceptable in some vegetarian diets. It all depends on the restrictions you set for yourself and what you consider acceptable. Alternative cheeses, milks, and eggs are interchangeable here, so feel free to tailor these ingredients to your dietary needs.

From Veggie Tortilla Wraps and Creamy Black Bean Taquitos to Tempeh "Steak" Bites and Fried Halloumi Caprese Salad, these recipes are not only filled with layers of flavors but have an added crispy texture, calling you to make them week after week. If you are someone who chooses to eat meat, don't be afraid to switch things up and dip your toes into the vegetarian waters. Swapping out some of your meals for options in this chapter can be good for your health and the environment, and they're just plain delicious!

Veggie Tortilla Wraps

These wraps are for those on the run. Just a few flips and a quick cook time, and you'll be on your way. If you want to add to this simple dish, spread a little mustard or mayonnaise to one of the quarters. Otherwise, put them together and be on your way.

Hands-On Time: 15 minutes
Cook Time: 4 minutes
Preheat Temperature: 350°F
Preheat Time: 3 minutes
Accessories/Prep: Fryer basket lined with aluminum foil

Serves 4

4 (8") flour tortillas
1 medium avocado, peeled, pitted, and mashed
12 slices English cucumber
½ cup shredded vegan mozzarella
8 slices jarred roasted red peppers, drained

WHAT IS AN ENGLISH CUCUMBER?

English cucumbers are longer and a little sweeter than the traditional cucumber. The skin is thin and usually unwaxed, so peeling is unnecessary. Because of this fragile exterior, they are sold wrapped in plastic. Another benefit of this variety is that the seeds are practically unnoticeable.

1 Place 1 tortilla on a cutting surface. Using a sharp knife, make a cut from the center of the tortilla to the edge. Imagine dividing the tortilla into four sections with the cut facing toward you. To the bottom left quadrant, add one-fourth of the mashed avocado. To the top left quadrant, add 3 cucumber slices. To the upper right quadrant, add 2 tablespoons mozzarella. To the bottom right quadrant, add 2 slices roasted red peppers.

2 Fold tortilla as follows to form a triangle: Begin by folding the bottom left quadrant over the top left quadrant; then, proceeding clockwise, fold this triangle over the top right quadrant and finally down over the bottom right quadrant. Repeat with remaining tortillas and place in prepared fryer basket.

3 Cook 2 minutes. Flip tortilla wraps. Cook an additional 2 minutes. Transfer to a plate and serve warm.

PER SERVING

CALORIES: 254 | FAT: 10g | PROTEIN: 5g | SODIUM: 563mg | FIBER: 4g | CARBOHYDRATES: 34g | SUGAR: 3g

Creamy Black Bean Taquitos

Not all refried black beans are created equal. Some contain animal lard and even dairy, so read the labels before you buy a can. Make sure you know exactly what's in your chosen brand, even if you're not vegan or vegetarian.

Hands-On Time: 15 minutes
Cook Time: 8 minutes
Preheat Temperature: 350°F
Preheat Time: 3 minutes
Accessories/Prep: Fryer basket

Serves 4

1 cup vegetarian refried black beans
2 ounces cream cheese, room temperature
1 teaspoon ground cumin
½ cup crumbled queso fresco
16 (6") corn tortillas
Olive oil cooking spray

QUICK AVOCADO-RANCH DIP
To make this quick dipping sauce, simply blend 1 cup bottled ranch dressing, ½ mashed (peeled and pitted) avocado, and 1 teaspoon sriracha. Make ahead and refrigerate covered until ready to use.

1 In a medium bowl, combine refried beans, cream cheese, cumin, and queso fresco. Spread about 2 tablespoons mixture over each corn tortilla, then roll each tortilla tightly.

2 Place eight taquitos seam side down in fryer basket. Spray tops with cooking spray and cook 4 minutes. Transfer to a cooling rack and repeat with remaining taquitos.

3 Serve warm.

PER SERVING

CALORIES: 377 | FAT: 14g | PROTEIN: 11g | SODIUM: 455mg | FIBER: 9g | CARBOHYDRATES: 51g | SUGAR: 2g

Loaded Avocado Toast

Avocado toast is all the rage, but this recipe takes it up a notch. The tartness of the goat cheese and the freshness of the tomato balance beautifully with the smooth, earthy avocado and that sweet balsamic glaze. You'll find yourself reaching for this morning after morning.

Hands-On Time: 10 minutes
Cook Time: 5 minutes
Preheat Temperature: 350°F
Preheat Time: 3 minutes
Accessories/Prep: Fryer basket

Serves 2

1 medium avocado, peeled, pitted, and diced
1 medium clove garlic, peeled and minced
¼ teaspoon fresh lime juice
¼ teaspoon salt
2 slices thick-sliced whole-grain bread
1 medium Roma tomato, seeded and diced
¼ cup crumbled goat cheese
¼ teaspoon ground black pepper
2 teaspoons balsamic glaze

1 In a small bowl, using the back of a fork, press avocado, garlic, lime juice, and salt until combined.

2 Spread avocado mixture over bread slices. Add tomato. Sprinkle with goat cheese and pepper.

3 Place topped bread in fryer basket. Cook 5 minutes. Transfer to a plate. Drizzle each piece of toast with balsamic glaze. Serve warm.

PER SERVING

CALORIES: 298 | FAT: 15g | PROTEIN: 10g | SODIUM: 511mg | FIBER: 8g | CARBOHYDRATES: 30g | SUGAR: 8g

WHAT IS BALSAMIC GLAZE?

It is a reduced and thicker form of balsamic vinegar. Although it can be purchased already reduced, don't you dare! It is so very easy to make. All you need is balsamic vinegar and a small pot. Simmer vinegar about 15 minutes until reduced to a thick sauce. Let cool and drizzle away!

Chili-Topped Sweet Potatoes

Whether your chili is leftover or canned, it doesn't matter. You can spoon it into a baked sweet potato for your next meal. Top it with some melty Cheddar cheese, chopped green onions, butter, or sour cream. Or better yet, add them all!

Hands-On Time: 10 minutes
Cook Time: 46 minutes
Preheat Temperature: 400°F
Preheat Time: 3 minutes
Accessories/Prep: Fryer basket

Serves 2

2 large sweet potatoes (about 1 pound)
2 teaspoons olive oil
2 cups vegetarian chili
1/2 cup shredded vegan Cheddar cheese

1 Using a fork, prick potatoes about five times each. Rub oil over both potatoes and place in fryer basket. Cook 30 minutes. Flip potatoes and cook an additional 15 minutes.

2 Meanwhile, heat chili in a small saucepan over medium-high heat for 4–5 minutes until heated through.

3 Transfer potatoes to a serving plate. Slice down the middle and top with chili and Cheddar. Place in air fryer and cook 1 additional minute. Serve warm.

PER SERVING

CALORIES: 421 | FAT: 12g | PROTEIN: 13g | SODIUM: 1,121mg | FIBER: 15g | CARBOHYDRATES: 67g | SUGAR: 11g

Acorn Squash Boats

This is the perfect recipe to turn to when your local produce section is filled with many different sizes and colors of squash. The following is a recipe for the more familiar acorn squash, but don't be afraid to spread your wings and air fry other varieties.

Hands-On Time: 10 minutes
Cook Time: 35 minutes
Preheat Temperature: 400°F
Preheat Time: 3 minutes
Accessories/Prep: Fryer basket

Serves 2

1 large acorn squash, halved and seeded
2 teaspoons unsalted butter, melted
2 teaspoons packed light brown sugar
$1/8$ teaspoon ground cinnamon
$1/8$ teaspoon ground nutmeg
$1/8$ teaspoon salt

1 Slice off about $1/4$" from bottom of each halved squash so it can sit flat as a bowl.

2 In a small bowl, combine butter, brown sugar, cinnamon, nutmeg, and salt. Brush mixture over top of squash halves and pour any remaining mixture into the hollow of squash halves.

3 Place acorn squash in fryer basket and cook 35 minutes. Transfer to two plates. Serve warm.

PER SQUASH BOAT

CALORIES: 165 | FAT: 4g | PROTEIN: 2g | SODIUM: 154mg | FIBER: 9g | CARBOHYDRATES: 35g | SUGAR: 4g

Tempeh "Steak" Bites

Tempeh is a dense, soy-based fermented product that really takes on the flavor of your marinade. The ingredient list looks long, but most of these ingredients can likely be found in your pantry. For a quick hack, use 1½ tablespoons of Montreal Steak Seasoning plus 1 teaspoon of Dijon mustard in lieu of the dry ingredients. It's close in flavor and will do the trick!

Hands-On Time: 10 minutes
Cook Time: 4 hours 15 minutes
Preheat Temperature: 350°F
Preheat Time: 3 minutes
Accessories/Prep: Fryer basket lined with parchment paper

Serves 2

2 tablespoons soy sauce
2 tablespoons vegan Worcestershire sauce
1 tablespoon olive oil
1 tablespoon water
½ teaspoon dried dill
½ teaspoon ground cumin
½ teaspoon ground mustard
½ teaspoon garlic powder
½ teaspoon red pepper flakes
½ teaspoon smoked paprika
½ teaspoon salt
1 (8-ounce) package tempeh, boiled and sliced into 1" pieces

1   In a quart-sized resealable plastic bag, add soy sauce, Worcestershire sauce, oil, water, dill, cumin, ground mustard, garlic powder, red pepper flakes, paprika, and salt. Add tempeh and toss to coat. Refrigerate 4 hours up to overnight, turning bag several times.

2   Place marinated tempeh in prepared fryer basket and cook 5 minutes. Flip and cook an additional 10 minutes.

3   Transfer to a plate and serve warm.

PER SERVING

CALORIES: 225 | FAT: 11g | PROTEIN: 21g | SODIUM: 172mg | FIBER: 0g | CARBOHYDRATES: 11g | SUGAR: 0g

Sticky Zucchini Fries

What's better than French fries? The answer is fries that are actually full of vegetables and make you feel great! Once again, the air fryer performs its magic with these crispy, crunchy dippers that satisfy and delight while providing important nutrients.

Hands-On Time: 10 minutes
Cook Time: 20 minutes
Preheat Temperature: 380°F
Preheat Time: 3 minutes
Accessories/Prep: Fryer basket sprayed with olive oil cooking spray

Serves 2

- ⅓ cup all-purpose flour
- 3 teaspoons cayenne pepper, divided
- ½ teaspoon salt
- 1 large egg
- 1 tablespoon water
- ½ cup panko bread crumbs
- 1 large zucchini, trimmed and cut into ¼" fries
- 2 tablespoons honey

1 In a small bowl, combine flour, 1½ teaspoons cayenne, and salt. In a second small bowl, whisk together egg and water. In a third small bowl, place bread crumbs.

2 Dredge 1 zucchini piece in flour mixture. Shake off excess flour, then dip in egg mixture. Shake off excess egg and dredge in bread crumbs. Shake off excess bread crumbs. Transfer to a plate and repeat with remaining zucchini. Place half of zucchini in prepared fryer basket and cook 5 minutes. Flip zucchini and cook an additional 5 minutes. Transfer fries to a medium serving dish and repeat with remaining zucchini.

3 In a clean small bowl, combine remaining cayenne and honey. Brush on cooked zucchini fries. Serve warm.

PER SERVING

CALORIES: 240 | **FAT:** 3g | **PROTEIN:** 8g | **SODIUM:** 366mg | **FIBER:** 2g | **CARBOHYDRATES:** 48g | **SUGAR:** 22g

Crispy Tofu and Broccoli over Quinoa

This is just like takeout but at half the cost and with the added bonus that you control the ingredients. But, for fun, you can serve this meal in Chinese takeout boxes along with some chopsticks. The boxes can be found online or in craft stores.

Hands-On Time: 15 minutes
Cook Time: 12 minutes
Preheat Temperature: 350°F
Preheat Time: 3 minutes
Accessories/Prep: Fryer basket sprayed with olive oil cooking spray

Serves 4

- 1 teaspoon sesame oil
- 1 teaspoon rice vinegar
- 1 teaspoon soy sauce
- 1/2 teaspoon Chinese five-spice powder
- 1/2 teaspoon chili powder
- 8 ounces extra-firm tofu, drained and cut into 1" cubes
- 1 medium bunch broccoli, trimmed and chopped into 1/4" pieces
- 4 cups cooked quinoa
- 1 tablespoon toasted sesame seeds
- 1 medium lime, cut into 4 wedges

1 In a large bowl, whisk together oil, vinegar, soy sauce, five-spice powder, and chili powder. Add tofu and toss to coat. Using a slotted spoon, and reserving sesame oil mixture, place tofu in prepared fryer basket. Cook 6 minutes.

2 Add broccoli to sesame oil mixture. Using a slotted spoon, add broccoli to fryer basket with tofu. Cook an additional 6 minutes.

3 Divide quinoa evenly among four serving bowls. Top with cooked tofu and broccoli. Garnish with sesame seeds and lime wedges. Serve warm.

PER SERVING

CALORIES: 353 | FAT: 9g | PROTEIN: 19g | SODIUM: 147mg | FIBER: 10g | CARBOHYDRATES: 52g | SUGAR: 4g

Polenta Fries Nachos

To cut these "fries," you'll want to narrowly slice off the ends of the precooked polenta. Slice that in half and then into ½" fries. Once they're crispy, top them with all your favorite nacho fixings for a unique yet flavorful combo.

Hands-On Time: 10 minutes
Cook Time: 30 minutes
Preheat Temperature: 400°F
Preheat Time: 3 minutes
Accessories/Prep: Fryer basket lined with parchment paper

Serves 2

1 tablespoon olive oil

1 teaspoon ground cumin

1 (18-ounce) package cooked polenta, sliced into 40 fries

1 medium avocado, peeled, pitted, and diced

2 medium Roma tomatoes, seeded and diced

¼ cup drained and rinsed black beans

¼ cup shredded Cheddar cheese

2 tablespoons drained jarred sliced jalapeño peppers

¼ cup sliced black olives

¼ cup plain Greek yogurt

¼ cup chopped fresh cilantro

1 In a medium bowl, whisk together oil and cumin. Add polenta fries and toss to coat.

2 Place polenta fries in prepared fryer basket. Cook 15 minutes. Gently flip fries. Cook an additional 15 minutes. Transfer to a large serving platter.

3 Top polenta fries with avocado, tomatoes, beans, Cheddar, jalapeño slices, and olives. Dollop yogurt on top and garnish with cilantro. Serve immediately.

PER SERVING

CALORIES: 566 | FAT: 29g | PROTEIN: 18g | SODIUM: 1,278mg | FIBER: 11g | CARBOHYDRATES: 54g | SUGAR: 6g

Sesame Eggplant

Like mushrooms, eggplant is one of those "meaty" vegetarian options. Add this eggplant atop a bowl of quinoa or alongside the Bulgogi Cauliflower Bites found in this chapter.

Hands-On Time: 10 minutes
Cook Time: 16 minutes
Preheat Temperature: 380°F
Preheat Time: 3 minutes
Accessories/Prep: Fryer basket

Serves 4

2 tablespoons sesame oil
1 teaspoon honey
1/8 teaspoon salt
1/8 teaspoon cayenne pepper
1/2 teaspoon dried basil
1 medium eggplant, trimmed
   and diced into 1" cubes

1 In a large bowl, combine oil, honey, salt, cayenne, and basil. Add eggplant cubes and toss to coat.

2 Place eggplant in fryer basket and cook 8 minutes. Shake basket and cook an additional 8 minutes.

3 Transfer eggplant to a dish. Serve warm.

PER SERVING

CALORIES: 99 | FAT: 7g | PROTEIN: 1g | SODIUM: 75mg | FIBER: 4g | CARBOHYDRATES: 10g | SUGAR: 6g

Island Vegan Hot Dogs

Hot dogs are not only for meat eaters. Mix it up with barbecue sauce and some pineapple and enjoy this vegan-friendly island combination!

Hands-On Time: 10 minutes
Cook Time: 9 minutes
Preheat Temperature: 400°F
Preheat Time: 3 minutes
Accessories/Prep: Fryer basket lined with parchment paper

Serves 4

1 (8-ounce) can pineapple
   chunks, drained
4 vegan hot dogs
4 hot dog buns
1/4 cup barbecue sauce,
   warmed
4 tablespoons diced red
   onion

1 Place drained pineapple in prepared fryer basket. Cook 4 minutes. Transfer pineapple to a bowl and discard parchment paper.

2 Place hot dogs in ungreased fryer basket and cook 4 minutes. Transfer hot dogs to hot dog buns. Return hot dogs in buns to fryer basket and cook an additional 1 minute.

3 Transfer hot dogs in buns to a large plate and top each with 1 tablespoon barbecue sauce, 1 tablespoon onion, and cooked pineapple. Serve immediately.

PER HOT DOG

CALORIES: 228 | FAT: 2g | PROTEIN: 12g | SODIUM: 824mg | FIBER: 3g | CARBOHYDRATES: 41g | SUGAR: 17g

Vegan Beans and Franks

Beans and franks may remind you of camping and cowboys, but you can make this meal anywhere you can plug in your air fryer. As long as you can find an electrical outlet, you're golden! It's totally fine to make them in your kitchen too.

Hands-On Time: 10 minutes
Cook Time: 9 minutes
Preheat Temperature: 400°F
Preheat Time: 3 minutes
Accessories/Prep: Fryer basket and cake barrel

Serves 4

- 1 (28-ounce) can vegetarian baked beans
- 1 teaspoon Dijon mustard
- 1 tablespoon packed light brown sugar
- 4 vegan hot dogs, each sliced into 6 pieces
- 4 tablespoons diced red onion

1 In a cake barrel, combine beans, mustard, brown sugar, and hot dog pieces. Place in fryer basket.

2 Cook 9 minutes. Remove barrel from fryer basket.

3 Divide franks and beans evenly among four bowls and garnish with red onion. Serve warm.

PER SERVING

CALORIES: 298 | FAT: 1g | PROTEIN: 18g | SODIUM: 1,332mg | FIBER: 7g | CARBOHYDRATES: 55g | SUGAR: 25g

South of the Border Loaded Avocados

Avocados can be considered nature's mayonnaise, lending a luxurious creaminess to anything you add it to. Full of vitamins, it's a healthier option than mayonnaise, and once you start subbing it in, you'll never stop. In this recipe, avocados are the star of the show.

Hands-On Time: 10 minutes
Cook Time: 5 minutes
Preheat Temperature: 400°F
Preheat Time: 3 minutes
Accessories/Prep: Fryer basket

Serves 2

- 2 large avocados, halved and pitted
- 1/4 cup drained and rinsed black beans
- 1/4 cup corn kernels
- 1 medium Roma tomato, seeded and diced small
- 4 tablespoons shredded Cheddar cheese
- 4 teaspoons plain Greek yogurt
- 2 tablespoons chopped fresh cilantro
- 1 teaspoon ground cumin
- 1/4 teaspoon salt

1 Scoop flesh out of avocado halves, reserving shells. Add avocado to a medium bowl and mash with the back of a fork until fairly smooth. Fold in beans, corn, and tomato.

2 Fill avocado shells with mixture. Top each with 1 tablespoon Cheddar. Place in fryer basket and cook 5 minutes.

3 Transfer avocados to plates. Top each half with 1 teaspoon yogurt and sprinkle with cilantro, cumin, and salt. Serve warm.

PER SERVING

CALORIES: 346 | FAT: 24g | PROTEIN: 10g | SODIUM: 469mg | FIBER: 12g | CARBOHYDRATES: 22g | SUGAR: 3g

Fried Halloumi Caprese Salad

Who knew that anything could compare to the angelic buffalo mozzarella in this southern Italian specialty? Halloumi crisps up so nicely and pairs beautifully with the freshness of the tomatoes, basil, olive oil, and balsamic vinegar. Don't forget to serve this with some artisanal bread.

Hands-On Time: 10 minutes
Cook Time: 10 minutes
Preheat Temperature: 350°F
Preheat Time: 3 minutes
Accessories/Prep: Fryer basket sprayed with olive oil cooking spray

Serves 4

- 2 tablespoons olive oil, divided
- 8 ounces Halloumi cheese, cut into ½" slices
- 2 medium Roma tomatoes, sliced
- 1 tablespoon balsamic vinegar
- ¼ cup chiffonade of fresh basil

FRESH BASIL CHIFFONADE
For a beautiful presentation and flavorful impact, simply stack the basil leaves one on top of the other before rolling them up. While they are rolled into a cigar-like shape, use a sharp knife to thinly slice. This will create long ribbons of basil when unrolled.

1 Brush 2 teaspoons oil over Halloumi slices.

2 Place Halloumi in prepared fryer basket. Cook 10 minutes until golden brown.

3 Divide Halloumi slices evenly among four plates. Add tomato slices in between Halloumi slices. Drizzle with remaining oil and vinegar. Garnish with basil. Serve immediately.

PER SERVING

CALORIES: 257 | FAT: 21g | PROTEIN: 12g | SODIUM: 569mg | FIBER: 0g | CARBOHYDRATES: 4g | SUGAR: 3g

Vegetarian Personal Pizza

Make this personal pizza, well, personal! If you are vegan, sub some dairy-free mozzarella shreds in place of the cheese. Also, you can add the tomatoes either before or after cooking the pizza. Both ways are tasty, but they give a different finish.

Hands-On Time: 10 minutes
Cook Time: 15 minutes
Preheat Temperature: 275°F
Preheat Time: 3 minutes
Accessories/Prep: Fryer basket; pizza pan sprayed with cooking spray

Serves 1

- $1/4$ pound fresh pizza dough
- 2 tablespoons marinara sauce
- 2 tablespoons sliced mushrooms
- 2 tablespoons chopped black olives
- 2 tablespoons diced green bell pepper
- 2 tablespoons diced red onion
- 1 medium Roma tomato, sliced
- $1/4$ cup shredded part-skim mozzarella cheese

1 Press out dough to fit prepared pizza pan. Place pan in fryer basket and cook 5 minutes.

2 Remove pan and spread marinara over dough up to $1/4$" from the edge. Evenly distribute mushrooms, olives, bell pepper, and onion over marinara. Place sliced tomatoes over pizza and sprinkle with mozzarella. Place pan in fryer basket and cook an additional 10 minutes.

3 Gently transfer pizza to a cutting board. Slice and serve.

PER SERVING

CALORIES: 414 | **FAT:** 11g | **PROTEIN:** 16g | **SODIUM:** 1,092mg | **FIBER:** 4g | **CARBOHYDRATES:** 65g | **SUGAR:** 12g

Garden-Stuffed Mushrooms

These tasty shrooms are hard to put down. The warm cheese, the bite of the onion, and the sweet and charred flavor of the red peppers make this combination a winner. The air fryer does its job cooking the outside of the mushrooms while making everything inside soft and creamy.

Hands-On Time: 10 minutes
Cook Time: 6 minutes
Preheat Temperature: 350°F
Preheat Time: 3 minutes
Accessories/Prep: Fryer basket

Serves 2

1 teaspoon olive oil
12 whole white button mushroom tops (about 10 ounces), stems removed
3 ounces cream cheese, room temperature
1 tablespoon grated yellow onion
2 tablespoons drained jarred finely diced roasted red peppers
4 medium fresh basil leaves, chopped
$1/8$ teaspoon salt
2 tablespoons panko bread crumbs

1 Brush oil around top ridge of each mushroom cap.

2 In a small bowl, combine cream cheese, onion, red peppers, basil, and salt. Divide mixture evenly and press into mushroom caps. Sprinkle bread crumbs on top.

3 Place stuffed mushrooms in fryer basket. Cook 6 minutes. Transfer to a plate and serve warm.

PER SERVING

CALORIES: 218 | FAT: 15g | PROTEIN: 7g | SODIUM: 391mg | FIBER: 1g | CARBOHYDRATES: 11g | SUGAR: 5g

Portobello Sandwiches

These sandwiches explode with flavor and texture. You will get some "meatiness" from the portobello mushroom, crunchiness from the cucumbers, and freshness from the sprouts and tomatoes. The pretzel bun is just one choice, as ciabatta, potato buns, and sesame buns are equally delicious here!

Hands-On Time: 10 minutes
Cook Time: 10 minutes
Preheat Temperature: 350°F
Preheat Time: 3 minutes
Accessories/Prep: Fryer basket

Serves 2

2 large portobello mushroom caps, stems removed and black gills scraped out

1 teaspoon olive oil

2 pretzel-style brioche hamburger buns

2 tablespoons mayonnaise

1 tablespoon Dijon mustard

2 slices beefsteak tomato

8 slices cucumber

1/4 cup broccoli sprouts

4 slices jarred roasted red peppers, drained

1 Brush tops of mushrooms with oil.

2 Place mushrooms in fryer basket and cook 8 minutes. Transfer to a plate. Place split buns in fryer basket and cook an additional 2 minutes.

3 Spread mayonnaise and mustard on buns and layer each with portobello, tomato, cucumber, sprouts, and peppers to make two sandwiches. Serve warm.

PER SANDWICH

CALORIES: 484 | FAT: 18g | PROTEIN: 12g | SODIUM: 968mg | FIBER: 4g | CARBOHYDRATES: 67g | SUGAR: 14g

Italian-Stuffed Large Portobellos

These are almost like low-carb pizzas, with the mushrooms taking the place of the crust. Don't forget to scrape out the black gills before filling your portobellos. After that, the Italian cheeses and flavors have room to sing!

Hands-On Time: 15 minutes
Cook Time: 8 minutes
Preheat Temperature: 350°F
Preheat Time: 3 minutes
Accessories/Prep: Fryer basket

Serves 2

2 large portobello mushrooms, stems removed and black gills scraped out
1 teaspoon olive oil
2 tablespoons marinara
1/4 cup whole-milk ricotta cheese
1/4 cup shredded part-skim mozzarella cheese
2 tablespoons grated Parmesan cheese
2 tablespoons chopped fresh basil
2 tablespoons grated yellow onion
2 tablespoons Italian-style bread crumbs

WHY DO YOU SCRAPE THE BLACK GILLS FROM PORTOBELLO CAPS?
Although edible, the black gills tend to hide dirt or sand, sometimes lending a gritty texture to your meal. Also, they can color the sauce or filling a murky brown, which can give an unappetizing appearance.

1   Brush tops of mushrooms with oil. Spoon marinara sauce into each mushroom.

2   In a small bowl, combine ricotta, mozzarella, Parmesan, basil, and onion. Distribute equally between mushroom caps. Top with bread crumbs.

3   Place stuffed mushrooms in fryer basket and cook 8 minutes. Transfer to a plate and serve warm.

PER SERVING

CALORIES: 186 | FAT: 10g | PROTEIN: 11g | SODIUM: 351mg | FIBER: 2g | CARBOHYDRATES: 13g | SUGAR: 4g

Spaghetti Squash Pizza Boats

This squash is a favorite because it resembles spaghetti noodles. It offers all the fun of twirling your fork without overloading on carbs. This recipe is even more like a pasta dish with the addition of marinara sauce and mozzarella.

Hands-On Time: 15 minutes
Cook Time: 27 minutes
Preheat Temperature: 375°F
Preheat Time: 3 minutes
Accessories/Prep: Fryer basket

Serves 2

- 2 teaspoons olive oil
- 1 (2-pound) spaghetti squash, halved and seeded
- ½ teaspoon salt
- 1 cup marinara sauce, warmed
- ½ cup shredded part-skim mozzarella cheese
- 1 tablespoon chopped parsley

1 Rub oil over cut sides of spaghetti squash. Season with salt. Place squash halves cut side down in fryer basket and cook 25 minutes. If squash is too wide, set halves up along the sides of the basket.

2 Transfer squash to a cutting board and let cool 10 minutes until easy to handle. Using a fork, gently scoop squash "noodles" into a medium bowl. Toss in marinara sauce and return noodles to squash halves. Top with mozzarella.

3 Return halves to fryer basket and cook 2 minutes or until mozzarella has melted. Sprinkle chopped parsley evenly over each pizza boat. Serve warm.

PER PIZZA BOAT

CALORIES: 181 | FAT: 6g | PROTEIN: 8g | SODIUM: 1,315mg | FIBER: 5g | CARBOHYDRATES: 24g | SUGAR: 13g

Goat Cheese Medallions

Served on a fresh green salad or on your next fancy charcuterie tray, these medallions are a game changer. Who knew goat cheese could be made even creamier than its original state? The air fryer not only warms the cheesy inside but also crisps up the outside.

Hands-On Time: 15 minutes
Cook Time: 8 minutes
Preheat Temperature: 350°F
Preheat Time: 3 minutes
Accessories/Prep: Fryer basket lined with aluminum foil

Serves 2

¼ cup all-purpose flour
¼ cup whole milk
¼ cup Italian-style bread crumbs
1 teaspoon salt
1 (4-ounce) log goat cheese, sliced into 4 rounds
1 tablespoon olive oil, divided

1 Place flour and milk in two separate shallow bowls. In a third shallow bowl, combine bread crumbs and salt. Press each goat cheese round into a ½"-thick circle.

2 Dredge 1 goat cheese round in flour. Shake off excess flour, then dip in milk. Shake off excess milk and dredge in bread crumbs. Shake off excess bread crumbs. Transfer to a plate and repeat with remaining rounds. Place cheese in prepared fryer basket and lightly brush tops with ½ tablespoon oil.

3 Cook 4 minutes. Flip slices and lightly brush tops with remaining oil. Cook an additional 4 minutes. Transfer cheese to a plate and serve warm.

PER SERVING

CALORIES: 359 | **FAT:** 24g | **PROTEIN:** 16g | **SODIUM:** 441mg | **FIBER:** 1g | **CARBOHYDRATES:** 17g | **SUGAR:** 2g

Bulgogi Cauliflower Bites

These cauliflower bites are reminiscent of a Korean barbecue joint. To round out the traditional feel, serve with sides such as kimchi, noodles, roasted eggplant, bean sprouts, a fried egg, or even sliced radishes. And don't forget to add a few squirts of gochujang sauce for a little kick.

Hands-On Time: 10 minutes
Cook Time: 7 minutes
Preheat Temperature: 350°F
Preheat Time: 3 minutes
Accessories/Prep: Fryer basket

Serves 4

- 1 large head cauliflower, cored and chopped into florets
- 2 teaspoons olive oil
- ¼ cup bulgogi sauce
- 2 medium scallions, trimmed and thinly sliced (green and white parts included)
- 2 teaspoons toasted sesame seeds

1. In a large bowl, toss cauliflower florets with oil.

2. Place cauliflower in fryer basket and cook 3 minutes. Shake fryer basket, then cook an additional 4 minutes. Transfer to a serving bowl.

3. Toss with bulgogi sauce. Garnish with scallions and sesame seeds. Serve warm.

PER SERVING

CALORIES: 107 | FAT: 3g | PROTEIN: 4g | SODIUM: 403mg | FIBER: 5g | CARBOHYDRATES: 17g | SUGAR: 10g

TOASTING SESAME SEEDS

Although sesame seeds can be purchased already toasted, you can also toast them yourself to bring out their nutty side and add a little crunchy texture. Simply place seeds in a clean skillet over medium heat. Using a wooden spoon, move them around for a couple of minutes until they start to turn light brown. Remove from heat. Once cooled completely, store in an airtight container in the pantry for up to 6 months.

Cinnamon, Maple, and Sage Butternut Squash

This beautifully sweet squash is enhanced by the sweetness of the maple syrup, while the cinnamon and sage bring an earthy tone. The salt and the chili powder not only accentuate the sweetness but they work double duty by adding a savory element that balances this dish.

Hands-On Time: 10 minutes
Cook Time: 20 minutes
Preheat Temperature: 375°F
Preheat Time: 3 minutes
Accessories/Prep: Fryer basket

Serves 6

2 tablespoons olive oil
2 tablespoons maple syrup
1 teaspoon ground cinnamon
$1/8$ teaspoon chili powder
$1/2$ teaspoon salt
1 medium butternut squash, peeled, seeded, and diced into 1" cubes
1 tablespoon chopped fresh sage

1 In a large bowl, whisk together oil, syrup, cinnamon, chili powder, and salt. Add diced squash and toss to coat.

2 Place squash in fryer basket. Cook 20 minutes, flipping every 5 minutes.

3 Transfer squash to a serving dish and garnish with fresh sage. Serve warm.

PER SERVING

CALORIES: 89 | FAT: 4g | PROTEIN: 1g | SODIUM: 198mg | FIBER: 3g | CARBOHYDRATES: 13g | SUGAR: 6g

Desserts

Desserts are the best, but sometimes we just want a little sweet treat without killing our ongoing diet or getting that sluggish feeling that comes after deep-fried or high-sugar foods. The air fryer is the perfect solution. There are so many different desserts and combinations you can put together with this appliance that can still be considered healthy—or at least healthier!

That's not to say you shouldn't indulge from time to time, and with these recipes you can do exactly that. Whether it is a nice ending to a family dinner, an after-school treat for the kiddos, or a midnight craving, there is something here for everyone.

From Staycation S'mores! and Cherry-Kissed Ricotta Mini Cheesecakes to Nutty Apple Pie Eggrolls and Strawberry Shortcake with Sweet Biscuits, this chapter is sure to cover all your sweet tooth cravings.

Mega Dark Chocolate–Mint Cookie

Sure, you could have a few regular-sized cookies. But why would you do that when you can have a mega cookie? A Mega Dark Chocolate–Mint Cookie at that! Enjoy it all to yourself or share it with someone special.

Hands-On Time: 10 minutes
Cook Time: 8 minutes
Preheat Temperature: 350°F
Preheat Time: 3 minutes
Accessories/Prep: Fryer basket; pizza pan sprayed with cooking spray

Serves 2

- $1/3$ cup all-purpose flour
- 2 tablespoons unsweetened dark cocoa
- 2 tablespoons granulated sugar
- 1 large egg, whisked
- $1/2$ teaspoon vanilla extract
- 3 tablespoons unsalted butter, melted
- $1/8$ teaspoon salt
- 2 tablespoons mint chips

1 In a medium bowl, combine all ingredients.

2 Spread mixture in prepared pizza pan. Place pan in fryer basket and cook 8 minutes.

3 Transfer to a serving plate and let cool 10 minutes. Slice and serve warm.

PER $1/2$ COOKIE

CALORIES: 399 | FAT: 24g | PROTEIN: 7g | SODIUM: 190mg | FIBER: 3g | CARBOHYDRATES: 40g | SUGAR: 20g

Caramelized Banana Sundaes

The air fryer softens an already sweet, delicious banana into a smooth and almost pudding-like consistency. Although this recipe calls for vanilla ice cream, use your favorite flavor. Peanut butter, cinnamon, and strawberry are three flavors that would pair well with this sundae's flavor profile.

Hands-On Time: 5 minutes
Cook Time: 4 minutes
Preheat Temperature: 370°F
Preheat Time: 3 minutes
Accessories/Prep: Fryer basket

Serves 2

- 1 banana, unpeeled and halved lengthwise
- 1/8 teaspoon ground cinnamon
- 4 teaspoons packed light brown sugar
- 2 scoops vanilla ice cream
- 1/4 cup chocolate sauce
- 1/3 cup whipped cream
- 2 maraschino cherries

1 Sprinkle banana halves with cinnamon and brown sugar. Place in fryer basket and cook 4 minutes. Transfer bananas to a plate and let rest 5 minutes until cool enough to handle.

2 Remove bananas from peel and divide evenly between two bowls.

3 Top caramelized bananas with ice cream, chocolate sauce, whipped cream, and cherries. Serve immediately.

PER SUNDAE

CALORIES: 391 | FAT: 13g | PROTEIN: 5g | SODIUM: 186mg | FIBER: 3g | CARBOHYDRATES: 64g | SUGAR: 45g

Baked Pears with Vanilla Ice Cream

This is such an easy dessert when you are craving something in a pinch. The air fryer softens the pears and brings out the natural sweetness. Plus, you never feel too guilty when desserts include fruit! You're still getting your share of nutrients this way.

Hands-On Time: 5 minutes
Cook Time: 12 minutes
Preheat Temperature: 370°F
Preheat Time: 3 minutes
Accessories/Prep: Fryer basket

Serves 4

1 tablespoon salted butter, melted
2 pears, halved and cored
$\frac{1}{8}$ teaspoon ground cinnamon
4 teaspoons packed light brown sugar
2 cups vanilla ice cream

HOW DO YOU CORE A PEAR?
Once the pear is cut in half, simply use a melon baller to scoop out the seeds and core. Alternately, you can use a metal tablespoon to achieve the same result. This process leaves more pear flesh than using a traditional corer, and it's prettier too!

1 Brush butter over cut sides of pears. Evenly sprinkle cinnamon and brown sugar over halves.

2 Place pears cut side up in fryer basket. Cook 12 minutes.

3 Transfer pears to bowls and top with ice cream. Serve immediately.

PER SERVING

CALORIES: 229 | FAT: 10g | PROTEIN: 3g | SODIUM: 55mg | FIBER: 3g | CARBOHYDRATES: 34g | SUGAR: 27g

Birthday Dessert Bagel

Start your birthday with a celebratory spirit from the minute you wake up. The air fryer toasts bagels to perfection, and the toppings are limited only by your imagination. Don't forget the candle and make a wish!

Hands-On Time: 5 minutes
Cook Time: 4 minutes
Preheat Temperature: 370°F
Preheat Time: 3 minutes
Accessories/Prep: Fryer basket sprayed with olive oil cooking spray

Serves 1

1 blueberry bagel, halved
2 tablespoons vanilla frosting
2 teaspoons rainbow sprinkles

1 Place split bagel cut side up in prepared fryer basket. Cook 4 minutes.

2 Transfer bagel halves to a plate.

3 Spread bagel halves with frosting. Garnish with sprinkles. Serve immediately.

PER BAGEL

CALORIES: 454 | FAT: 8g | PROTEIN: 10g | SODIUM: 421mg | FIBER: 2g | CARBOHYDRATES: 88g | SUGAR: 35g

Staycation S'mores!

S'mores don't have to be shared around a flame. Pop a tent in the living room and then mosey into the kitchen and circle around the air fryer.

Hands-On Time: 5 minutes
Cook Time: 10 minutes
Preheat Temperature: 370°F
Preheat Time: 3 minutes
Accessories/Prep: Fryer basket

Serves 4

8 graham crackers, broken in half to create 16 squares
8 large marshmallows
2 (1.5-ounce) chocolate bars, broken into 2" pieces

1 Place 4 square crackers in fryer basket. Top each square with 1 marshmallow and cook 5 minutes. Check your marshmallow. Cook longer if necessary.

2 Transfer to a plate and top marshmallow with 1 piece of chocolate and a second square cracker. Repeat with remaining ingredients.

3 Serve immediately.

PER SERVING

CALORIES: 166 | FAT: 9g | PROTEIN: 4g | SODIUM: 157mg | FIBER: 1g | CARBOHYDRATES: 47g | SUGAR: 27g

Cherry-Kissed Ricotta Mini Cheesecakes

This is a great way to use the juice from those sundae cherries in your refrigerator door. The juice adds just a kiss of cherry flavor to this traditional Italian ricotta cheesecake. Serve with whipped cream and cherries on top for an added touch!

Hands-On Time: 15 minutes
Cook Time: 10 minutes
Preheat Temperature: 330°F
Preheat Time: 3 minutes
Accessories/Prep: Fryer basket

Serves 6

- 3 tablespoons cream cheese, room temperature
- 1 cup whole-milk ricotta cheese
- 4 tablespoons granulated sugar
- $1/4$ teaspoon vanilla extract
- 1 tablespoon juice from jarred maraschino cherries
- 2 large eggs, whisked
- $1/8$ teaspoon salt
- 6 (3") mini graham cracker piecrusts

1   In a medium bowl, combine cream cheese, ricotta, sugar, vanilla, cherry juice, eggs, and salt.

2   Distribute mixture evenly among piecrusts. Place in fryer basket. Cook 10 minutes.

3   Transfer to a cooling rack and let rest 1 hour. Refrigerate covered for at least 1 hour or overnight before serving chilled.

PER CHEESECAKE

CALORIES: 254 | FAT: 13g | PROTEIN: 8g | SODIUM: 203mg | FIBER: 0g | CARBOHYDRATES: 23g | SUGAR: 13g

Choose-Your-Flavor Cheesecake

Sour cream is often an ingredient in cheesecake recipes, but Greek yogurt is a great substitute. So choose your favorite flavor of Greek yogurt and change up this recipe every time! Whether it's strawberry, vanilla bean, coconut, key lime, or blueberry, it's sure to be delicious.

Hands-On Time: 15 minutes
Cook Time: 33 minutes
Preheat Temperature: 400°F
Preheat Time: 3 minutes
Accessories/Prep: Fryer basket and 7" springform pan

Serves 6

1 cup almond flour (or almond meal)
3 tablespoons unsalted butter, melted
1/4 cup packed light brown sugar
12 ounces cream cheese, room temperature
1 (5.3-ounce) container Greek yogurt
2 large eggs
1/4 cup granulated sugar
1/8 teaspoon salt
1 teaspoon vanilla extract

MONEY-SAVER TIP

Almond flour can be a little pricey, but you can make your own. It is simply almonds ground to the consistency of flour. Use a food processor or blender to achieve this. Also, you can use a variety of nuts such as pecans, walnuts, or pistachios for this crust!

1 In a medium bowl, combine almond flour, butter, and brown sugar. Press mixture into bottom and halfway up sides of springform pan. Place pan in fryer basket and cook 5 minutes. Remove from basket and allow to cool at least 30 minutes.

2 In a large bowl, combine remaining ingredients. Spoon mixture over cooled crust. Cover with aluminum foil. Return pan to fryer basket and cook 13 minutes.

3 Remove aluminum foil and reduce air fryer temperature to 350°F. Cook an additional 15 minutes. Refrigerate at least 2 hours to allow cheesecake to set. Once set, release sides of springform pan. Slice and serve chilled.

PER SERVING

CALORIES: 485 | FAT: 35g | PROTEIN: 12g | SODIUM: 290mg | FIBER: 2g | CARBOHYDRATES: 24g | SUGAR: 21g

Giant Oatmeal-Raisin Cookie

Oatmeal-raisin cookies can get a bad rap when stacked against their more popular variations, like chocolate chip or sugar. But in reality, they're just as delicious. If raisins don't appeal, swap them out for your choice of chocolate chips or just take them out altogether.

Hands-On Time: 10 minutes
Cook Time: 10 minutes
Preheat Temperature: 370°F
Preheat Time: 3 minutes
Accessories/Prep: Fryer basket; pizza pan sprayed with cooking spray

Serves 2

$1/3$ cup all-purpose flour
$1/3$ cup packed dark brown sugar
$1^1/2$ cups rolled oats
$1/2$ teaspoon ground cinnamon
1 large egg, whisked
$1/2$ teaspoon vanilla extract
3 tablespoons unsalted butter, melted
$1/8$ teaspoon salt
1 tablespoon diced raisins

1 In a medium bowl, combine all ingredients.

2 Spread mixture in prepared pizza pan. Place pan in fryer basket and cook 10 minutes.

3 Transfer to a serving plate and let cool 10 minutes. Slice and serve warm.

PER SERVING

CALORIES: 647 | FAT: 23g | PROTEIN: 13g | SODIUM: 193mg | FIBER: 7g | CARBOHYDRATES: 97g | SUGAR: 41g

Cinnamon-Sugar Palmiers

These crispy little French cookies are impressive to look at and are very easy to make. Because of their distinct shape, they are also known as pig's ears, palm leaves, and even shoe soles! Bring these to the next bake sale to turn some heads.

Hands-On Time: 15 minutes
Cook Time: 54 minutes
Preheat Temperature: 350°F
Preheat Time: 3 minutes
Accessories/Prep: Fryer basket lined with parchment paper

Serves 6

- ¼ cup plus 2 teaspoons turbinado sugar, divided
- 1 sheet thawed frozen phyllo dough, room temperature
- 1 tablespoon unsalted butter, melted
- ½ teaspoon ground cinnamon

1 On a flat, clean surface, sprinkle 2 teaspoons sugar. Place phyllo sheet over scattered sugar. Brush butter over sheet. Sprinkle with remaining sugar and cinnamon. Carefully roll one long end toward the middle of sheet. Stop at the halfway point. Roll opposite side toward the middle. Refrigerate 30 minutes.

2 Slice log into eighteen equal slices.

3 Place six palmiers in prepared fryer basket. Cook 8 minutes. Transfer cooked palmiers to a cooling rack, then repeat with remaining palmiers. Serve warm or at room temperature.

PER SERVING

CALORIES: 63 | FAT: 2g | PROTEIN: 0g | SODIUM: 15mg | FIBER: 0g | CARBOHYDRATES: 11g | SUGAR: 9g

Mixed Berry Jubilee Topping

This berrylicious topping can be made the day before being served, so it's great for busy people who are used to meal prepping. Serve it warm or chilled atop your morning oatmeal, as a snack with vanilla Greek yogurt, or as a rich topping for cheesecake.

Hands-On Time: 10 minutes
Cook Time: 9 minutes
Preheat Temperature: 350°F
Preheat Time: 3 minutes
Accessories/Prep: Fryer basket and cake barrel

Serves 4

2 tablespoons unsalted butter, melted
1/4 cup granulated sugar
2 teaspoons cornstarch
1 tablespoon freshly squeezed orange juice
1/2 teaspoon orange zest
1/8 teaspoon salt
2 cups frozen mixed berries

1 In a medium bowl, whisk together butter, sugar, cornstarch, orange juice, orange zest, and salt. Add berries and toss to coat. Pour into a cake barrel.

2 Place cake barrel in fryer basket. Cook 9 minutes, stirring every 3 minutes.

3 Transfer mixture to a bowl. If not using immediately, let cool completely before storing refrigerated in an airtight container for up to 3 days.

PER SERVING

CALORIES: 142 | FAT: 6g | PROTEIN: 1g | SODIUM: 73mg | FIBER: 3g | CARBOHYDRATES: 23g | SUGAR: 18g

Nutty Apple Pie Eggrolls

These easy-to-make yet delicious treats are something a little bit different and are great to serve around the holidays, when the family is gathered. So, after a festive dinner, break out these apple pie eggrolls with a pot of coffee for a happy group!

Hands-On Time: 20 minutes
Cook Time: 32 minutes
Preheat Temperature: 350°F
Preheat Time: 3 minutes
Accessories/Prep: Fryer basket lined with parchment paper

Serves 10

4 cups diced peeled Granny
    Smith apples
1 tablespoon lemon juice
1 tablespoon unsalted butter
2 tablespoons granulated
    sugar
2 tablespoons packed light
    brown sugar
1 teaspoon ground cinnamon
2 teaspoons cornstarch
2 tablespoons pecan bits
2 tablespoons water
1/8 teaspoon salt
10 eggroll wrappers
Butter-flavored cooking
    spray
2 tablespoons confectioners'
    sugar

1 In a medium saucepan over high heat, combine apples, lemon juice, butter, granulated sugar, brown sugar, cinnamon, cornstarch, pecan bits, water, and salt. Stir until everything is combined. Reduce heat to low and simmer covered 8 minutes. Let mixture cool completely.

2 Place 1 eggroll wrapper on a work surface. Place 2 tablespoons mixture in center of wrapper. Fold 1/2" of both ends of wrapper over mixture. Roll lengthwise to form an eggroll and transfer seam side down to a plate. Continue with remaining wrappers and filling.

3 Place five eggrolls in prepared fryer basket. Spray with cooking spray and cook 9 minutes. Flip eggrolls and cook 3 minutes. Transfer eggrolls to a cooling rack, seam side down. Repeat with remaining eggrolls. Dust with confectioners' sugar and serve warm or chilled.

PER EGGROLL

CALORIES: 162 | FAT: 2g | PROTEIN: 3g | SODIUM: 212mg | FIBER: 1g | CARBOHYDRATES: 32g | SUGAR: 11g

Carrot Cake with Cream Cheese Frosting

Moist and, well, moist. This cake is delicious. The warmth of the spices and the grated carrots make this traditional cake a dream. Add a simple cream cheese frosting as the perfect topping for a bite with a cup of tea.

Hands-On Time: 10 minutes
Cook Time: 30 minutes
Preheat Temperature: 350°F
Preheat Time: 3 minutes
Accessories/Prep: Fryer basket; pizza pan sprayed with cooking spray

Serves 4

- ½ cup self-rising flour
- ½ cup packed light brown sugar
- ½ teaspoon ground cinnamon
- ¼ teaspoon ground nutmeg
- ½ cup grated carrots
- ½ teaspoon vanilla extract
- ¼ cup unsalted butter, melted
- 1 large egg, whisked
- 3 tablespoons cream cheese, room temperature
- ¼ cup confectioners' sugar
- ½ teaspoon whole milk
- ¼ teaspoon vanilla extract

1 In a large bowl, combine flour, brown sugar, cinnamon, nutmeg, carrots, vanilla, butter, and egg. Pour into prepared pizza pan. Place pan in fryer basket and cook 30 minutes. Transfer to a cooling rack.

2 While cake is cooling, in a small bowl, whisk together cream cheese, confectioners' sugar, milk, and vanilla.

3 Once cake is completely cooled, flip onto a plate. Frost with cream cheese mixture. Slice and serve.

PER SERVING

CALORIES: 344 | FAT: 15g | PROTEIN: 4g | SODIUM: 250mg | FIBER: 1g | CARBOHYDRATES: 47g | SUGAR: 34g

Naked Coconut Cake

This cake is so good, it doesn't even need frosting. Have a slice after dinner with a cup of coffee (whether or not it's caffeinated is up to you). The coconut milk and flakes provide a little something different for dessert time.

Hands-On Time: 15 minutes
Cook Time: 25 minutes
Preheat Temperature: 350°F
Preheat Time: 3 minutes
Accessories/Prep: Fryer basket; 7" springform pan sprayed with cooking spray

Serves 6

- ¼ cup unsalted butter, melted and cooled
- ½ cup canned full-fat coconut milk
- ½ teaspoon vanilla extract
- 2 large eggs
- ½ cup sweetened coconut flakes
- ½ cup granulated sugar
- 1¼ cups all-purpose flour
- 2 teaspoons baking powder
- ½ teaspoon baking soda
- ⅛ teaspoon salt

1 In a medium bowl, whisk together butter, coconut milk, vanilla, and eggs. In a separate medium bowl, combine coconut flakes, sugar, flour, baking powder, baking soda, and salt. Add butter mixture to bowl with dry ingredients. Gently combine; do not overmix. Spoon mixture into prepared springform pan.

2 Place pan in fryer basket and cook 25 minutes.

3 Transfer pan to a cooling rack and let cool 15 minutes. Remove sides of pan. Slice and serve warm or at room temperature.

PER SERVING

CALORIES: 321 | FAT: 15g | PROTEIN: 5g | SODIUM: 136mg | FIBER: 1g | CARBOHYDRATES: 41g | SUGAR: 19g

Chocolate Chip and Pecan Mini Cakes

These chocolatey, nutty cakes are one of those last-minute desserts for a sudden sweet tooth or an unexpected guest. Perk up a cup of coffee or tea and serve this quick dessert for whatever or whoever is around!

Hands-On Time: 10 minutes
Cook Time: 12 minutes
Preheat Temperature: 350°F
Preheat Time: 3 minutes
Accessories/Prep: Fryer basket; 4 (6-ounce) ramekins sprayed with cooking spray

Serves 4

1 cup all-purpose flour
$1/3$ cup granulated sugar
1 teaspoon baking powder
$1/8$ teaspoon salt
1 teaspoon vanilla extract
$2/3$ cup whole milk
2 tablespoons pecan bits
2 tablespoons milk chocolate chips

1   In a large bowl, combine ingredients, but do not overmix.

2   Distribute batter evenly among prepared ramekins.

3   Place ramekins in fryer basket and cook 12 minutes. Remove from basket and let cool to room temperature. Serve.

PER MINI CAKE

CALORIES: 258 | FAT: 5g | PROTEIN: 5g | SODIUM: 216mg | FIBER: 1g | CARBOHYDRATES: 47g | SUGAR: 22g

Brownie in a Mug for One

If you feel that sweet tooth calling and you don't want to commit to an entire tray of brownies, make one for you in just minutes. Serve by itself or with a dollop of whipped cream or even ice cream. Add a tablespoon of crushed nuts or a pinch of cayenne pepper if you'd like. This is your treat!

Hands-On Time: 10 minutes
Cook Time: 13 minutes
Preheat Temperature: 400°F
Preheat Time: 3 minutes
Accessories/Prep: Fryer basket; 12-ounce oven-safe mug sprayed with cooking spray

Serves 1

¼ cup self-rising flour
2 tablespoons unsweetened cocoa
¼ cup granulated sugar
2 tablespoons semisweet chocolate chips
⅛ teaspoon salt
1 teaspoon vanilla extract
¼ cup whole milk

MAKE SOMEONE'S DAY!

Do you have a friend who needs a little pick-me-up? Here's an inexpensive way to tell someone you are thinking of them. Combine the dry ingredients of this recipe in a little baggie and place it inside a cute mug. Insert a little card telling them how to finish the treat.

1 In prepared mug, combine all ingredients.

2 Place mug in fryer basket and cook 13 minutes or until brownie is cooked through. Remove fryer basket and let mug cool 10 minutes.

3 Serve warm or cooled.

PER BROWNIE

CALORIES: 475 | FAT: 10g | PROTEIN: 7g | SODIUM: 670mg | FIBER: 6g | CARBOHYDRATES: 96g | SUGAR: 66g

Strawberry Shortcake with Sweet Biscuits

Fresh strawberries, cool whipped cream, and warm, flaky sweet biscuits are a winning trio. Make a double batch of the biscuits in the morning for breakfast and then enjoy this dessert again at the end of the day. They're perfect anytime!

Hands-On Time: 15 minutes
Cook Time: 9 minutes
Preheat Temperature: 350°F
Preheat Time: 3 minutes
Accessories/Prep: Fryer basket; pizza pan sprayed with cooking spray

Serves 4

2 cups sliced strawberries
1 tablespoon plus 2 teaspoons granulated sugar, divided
2 cups self-rising flour, plus extra for flouring hands
4 tablespoons cold salted butter, cubed small
1 cup whole buttermilk
2 cups whipped cream

1 In a small bowl, toss strawberries with 1 tablespoon granulated sugar. Set aside. In a medium bowl, combine flour, remaining granulated sugar, butter, and buttermilk until a sticky dough forms.

2 Flour your hands and form dough into eight balls. Place balls in prepared pizza pan. Biscuits will be touching. Place pan in fryer basket and cook 9 minutes.

3 Transfer biscuits to a cooling rack. Let cool 5 minutes before pulling apart. Slice biscuits in half, add to bowls, and garnish with strawberries. Top with whipped cream. Serve immediately.

PER SERVING

CALORIES: 446 | FAT: 17g | PROTEIN: 7g | SODIUM: 766mg | FIBER: 2g | CARBOHYDRATES: 63g | SUGAR: 16g

Peanut Butter and Banana Mug Cake

Peanut butter and bananas is a combination that's hard to get enough of. Enjoy this mug cake as is, or add some chocolate chips for an extra treat. Better yet, some crumbled bacon on top would really channel your inner Elvis.

Hands-On Time: 10 minutes
Cook Time: 13 minutes
Preheat Temperature: 400°F
Preheat Time: 3 minutes
Accessories/Prep: Fryer basket and 12-ounce oven-safe mug

Serves 1

1 small ripe banana, peeled and mashed
2 tablespoons self-rising flour
2 tablespoons packed light brown sugar
$1/8$ teaspoon salt
1 teaspoon vanilla extract
1 tablespoon vegetable oil
2 tablespoons whole milk
1 tablespoon creamy peanut butter

1 In a 12-ounce mug, combine all ingredients.

2 Place mug in fryer basket and cook 13 minutes or until cake is cooked through. Remove fryer basket and let mug cool 10 minutes.

3 Serve warm or cooled.

PER SERVING

CALORIES: 491 | FAT: 22g | PROTEIN: 7g | SODIUM: 487mg | FIBER: 4g | CARBOHYDRATES: 67g | SUGAR: 43g

Raspberry Cheesecake Bombs

These little delights require minimal items and work. They do, however, deliver big on taste! Don't feel like you need to be limited to raspberry when it comes to this recipe. Use whatever preserves or jam are in your refrigerator and play with the flavors.

Hands-On Time: 15 minutes
Cook Time: 15 minutes
Preheat Temperature: 320°F
Preheat Time: 3 minutes
Accessories/Prep: Fryer basket lined with parchment paper

Serves 8

1 (16.3-ounce) can refrigerated oversized biscuits (8 total)
2 ounces cream cheese, room temperature
¼ cup raspberry preserves
2 tablespoons confectioners' sugar

1 Open can of biscuits and separate on a cutting board. Roll out each biscuit into a circle about ¼" thick.

2 In a small bowl, combine cream cheese and preserves. Evenly distribute mixture among biscuits, spooning into center of each biscuit circle. Fold dough up to a point and pinch to seal. Place in prepared fryer basket seam side down.

3 Cook 15 minutes. Transfer to a cooling rack and let rest 5 minutes. Sprinkle with confectioners' sugar. Serve warm or chilled.

PER BOMB

CALORIES: 264 | FAT: 8g | PROTEIN: 4g | SODIUM: 607mg | FIBER: 2g | CARBOHYDRATES: 38g | SUGAR: 12g

Glazed Chocolate Chip Biscuit Bites

These are similar to doughnut holes, but without the excess doughnut. And they're as simple as adding the ingredients together and rolling them into these small bites. Most important, they are absolutely delicious.

Hands-On Time: 15 minutes
Cook Time: 9 minutes
Preheat Temperature: 350°F
Preheat Time: 3 minutes
Accessories/Prep: Fryer basket; pizza pan sprayed with cooking spray

Serves 4

2 cups self-rising flour, plus extra for flouring hands
1 teaspoon granulated sugar
4 tablespoons cold salted butter, cubed small
1 cup whole buttermilk
2 tablespoons mini semi-sweet chocolate chips
½ cup confectioners' sugar
1 tablespoon whole milk
⅛ teaspoon vanilla extract

1 In a medium bowl, combine flour, granulated sugar, butter, buttermilk, and chocolate chips until a sticky dough forms.

2 Flour your hands and form dough into eight balls. Place in prepared pizza pan. Biscuits will be touching. Place pan in fryer basket and cook 9 minutes. Transfer pan to a cooling rack and let cool 10 minutes.

3 In a separate medium bowl, whisk together confectioners' sugar, milk, and vanilla until smooth. Drizzle over cooled biscuits. Pull apart and serve warm or at room temperature.

PER SERVING

CALORIES: 422 | FAT: 14g | PROTEIN: 7g | SODIUM: 771mg | FIBER: 1g | CARBOHYDRATES: 64g | SUGAR: 19g

Ginger Candied Pecans

These pecans are delicious as a sweet and salty snack. But you can also add them to your charcuterie board beside a variety of cheeses and cured meats, or chopped up in a salad, where they'll lend texture and a gingery punch to your usual combination.

Hands-On Time: 10 minutes
Cook Time: 20 minutes
Preheat Temperature: 300°F
Preheat Time: 3 minutes
Accessories/Prep: Fryer basket lined with parchment paper

Serves 8

1 large egg white
1/2 teaspoon vanilla extract
1 teaspoon water
1/4 cup granulated sugar
1/4 cup packed light brown sugar
2 teaspoons ground ginger
1/2 teaspoon salt
2 cups pecan halves

1 In a small bowl, whisk egg white, vanilla, and water until frothy. In a separate medium bowl, combine granulated sugar, brown sugar, ginger, and salt.

2 Coat pecans in egg white mixture. Dredge in sugar mixture. Place in prepared fryer basket and cook 20 minutes, stirring every 5 minutes.

3 Transfer pecans to a plate, spread apart, and let cool 30 minutes. Eat immediately or transfer to an airtight container once completely cooled. Refrigerate for up to 2 weeks or at room temperature for 1 week.

PER SERVING

CALORIES: 225 | FAT: 17g | PROTEIN: 3g | SODIUM: 153mg | FIBER: 2g | CARBOHYDRATES: 17g | SUGAR: 14g

Candied Walnut Popcorn Party Bowl

This sweet snack is perfect for a family movie night, when everyone gathers around the television for a much-awaited film, or a family game night. Consider transferring this mix to several bowls so that everyone has their fill and nobody ends up fighting over the bowl!

Hands-On Time: 10 minutes
Cook Time: 20 minutes
Preheat Temperature: 300°F
Preheat Time: 3 minutes
Accessories/Prep: Fryer basket lined with parchment paper

Serves 8

1 large egg white
1/2 teaspoon vanilla extract
1 teaspoon water
1/4 cup granulated sugar
1/4 cup packed light brown sugar
2 teaspoons ground cinnamon
1/2 teaspoon salt
2 cups walnut halves
8 cups popped popcorn
1/2 cup raisins
1/2 cup candy-coated chocolates

1 In a medium bowl, whisk egg white, vanilla, and water until frothy. In a separate medium bowl, combine granulated sugar, brown sugar, cinnamon, and salt.

2 Coat walnuts in egg white mixture. Dredge in sugar mixture. Place in prepared fryer basket and cook 20 minutes, stirring every 5 minutes.

3 Transfer walnuts to a plate, spread apart, and let cool 30 minutes. In a large bowl, add walnuts, popcorn, raisins, and candy-coated chocolates. Toss to combine. Serve.

PER SERVING

CALORIES: 352 | FAT: 20g | PROTEIN: 6g | SODIUM: 163mg | FIBER: 4g | CARBOHYDRATES: 39g | SUGAR: 28g

US/Metric Conversion Chart

VOLUME CONVERSIONS

US Volume Measure	Metric Equivalent
⅛ teaspoon	0.5 milliliter
¼ teaspoon	1 milliliter
½ teaspoon	2 milliliters
1 teaspoon	5 milliliters
½ tablespoon	7 milliliters
1 tablespoon (3 teaspoons)	15 milliliters
2 tablespoons (1 fluid ounce)	30 milliliters
¼ cup (4 tablespoons)	60 milliliters
⅓ cup	90 milliliters
½ cup (4 fluid ounces)	125 milliliters
⅔ cup	160 milliliters
¾ cup (6 fluid ounces)	180 milliliters
1 cup (16 tablespoons)	250 milliliters
1 pint (2 cups)	500 milliliters
1 quart (4 cups)	1 liter (about)

WEIGHT CONVERSIONS

US Weight Measure	Metric Equivalent
½ ounce	15 grams
1 ounce	30 grams
2 ounces	60 grams
3 ounces	85 grams
¼ pound (4 ounces)	115 grams
½ pound (8 ounces)	225 grams
¾ pound (12 ounces)	340 grams
1 pound (16 ounces)	454 grams

OVEN TEMPERATURE CONVERSIONS

Degrees Fahrenheit	Degrees Celsius
200 degrees F	95 degrees C
250 degrees F	120 degrees C
275 degrees F	135 degrees C
300 degrees F	150 degrees C
325 degrees F	160 degrees C
350 degrees F	180 degrees C
375 degrees F	190 degrees C
400 degrees F	205 degrees C
425 degrees F	220 degrees C
450 degrees F	230 degrees C

BAKING PAN SIZES

American	Metric
8 x 1½ inch round baking pan	20 x 4 cm cake tin
9 x 1½ inch round baking pan	23 x 3.5 cm cake tin
11 x 7 x 1½ inch baking pan	28 x 18 x 4 cm baking tin
13 x 9 x 2 inch baking pan	30 x 20 x 5 cm baking tin
2 quart rectangular baking dish	30 x 20 x 3 cm baking tin
15 x 10 x 2 inch baking pan	30 x 25 x 2 cm baking tin (Swiss roll tin)
9 inch pie plate	22 x 4 or 23 x 4 cm pie plate
7 or 8 inch springform pan	18 or 20 cm springform or loose bottom cake tin
9 x 5 x 3 inch loaf pan	23 x 13 x 7 cm or 2 lb narrow loaf or pate tin
1½ quart casserole	1.5 liter casserole
2 quart casserole	2 liter casserole

Index

Note: Page numbers in **bold** indicate recipe category lists.

About the Author

Michelle Fagone is a recipe developer and food blogger. On her site, CavegirlCuisine.com, she shares recipes and knowledge about the health benefits of cooking with local, fresh, nonprocessed foods. *Cavegirl Cuisine* has been honored by the Institute for the Psychology of Eating. Michelle is the author of numerous cookbooks, including *The "I Love My Instant Pot®" Recipe Book*, *The "I Love My Air Fryer" Low-Carb Recipe Book*, *The "I Love My Air Fryer" Gluten-Free Recipe Book*, and *The Everything® Air Fryer Cookbook*. She lives in Louisville, Kentucky.

Quick, easy, & delicious recipes, using 5 INGREDIENTS or less!

THE
"I LOVE MY
AIR
FRYER"
5-Ingredient
RECIPE BOOK

From *French Toast Sticks* to
Buttermilk-Fried Chicken Thighs,
175 Quick and Easy Recipes

Robin Fields

PICK UP OR DOWNLOAD YOUR COPY TODAY!

adamsmedia
An Imprint of Simon & Schuster
A Paramount Company